To Lead is to Serve

To Gurumayi Chidvilasananda
with gratitude for showing me the joyousness
in all of God's creation.

To Lead is to Serve

HOW TO ATTRACT VOLUNTEERS & KEEP THEM

Shar McBee

Design by Kathie Kemp
Cover design by Marjorie Corbett
Copyright © 1994, Shar McBee

Library of Congress No. TXU 574 712
ISBN 0-9638560-0-6

My grateful appreciation
to all the volunteer leaders and friends
who shared their advice and encouragement, to
Gabriele Lopez-Watermann for boundless inspiration, to
Catherine Kekoa Enomoto for being my writing partner,
to screenwriters David Walter and Collin Chang for boun-
tiful assistance with the computer and advertising,
to Hattie Whitaker for being a great landlord and "editor"
and to Kathie Kemp for really knowing what she was doing.

Contents

CONTINUED

Before You
Begin

Before you begin:

To Lead Is To Serve : How to Attract Volunteers & Keep Them is for leaders who work with volunteers. It is for people with big hearts and high hopes who want to give of themselves to the world.

To Lead Is To Serve is about an ancient leadership principle and also the nuts and bolts of how to attract volunteers and keep them. The work of influencing people can only be gradual. Sudden influences never endure. For this reason, the information in this book is designed to be embraced gradually, step by step, so that the effects will be lasting. As soon as you apply the basic principle, you will begin to see results. Later, take the other steps, adding a new one each month. In one year your organization can be transformed.

One word of warning: None of the techniques can be applied once. Like brushing your teeth, they must become a daily routine.

Professionally, I was a teacher of the physically challenged and then a journalist. I began volunteering when I was eight years old, answering the telephone at my church. I loved it and continued to volunteer throughout my life but I had never been in charge of any co-workers until I volunteered for a large foundation where, after a few years, I found myself supervising up to 500 people. Many of them spoke languages different from my own. The foundation sponsors programs and seminars on seven continents in over fifty countries. We travelled all over the world, often arriving in a country only a few days before an enormous event. We had to find out where the program was, where the hundreds of volunteers and staff were, meet with them, train them and then open the doors.

There was a wonderful supervisor who encouraged us to never do less than our best. No matter how "impossible" things seem, you must still give your all. Long before I had heard of quality management, I was being stretched beyond imagination as I went from supervising no one to supervising people from pay phones or hotel room offices around the world. I could not believe this had happened to me and I was continually amazed at how it worked. Years later, I was introduced to the idea *To Lead Is To Serve* and thought, "That's the secret! In order to lead people, we must learn to serve them."

While I was a journalist, I had always had an "attitude" toward public relations people. We journalists thought we were superior to them because we told the "truth" while they "sold" their clients. So you can imagine how dismayed I was when my supervisor expanded my duties to include overseeing public relations. That was the last thing I wanted to do. I actually cringed at the thought. Nonetheless, I began doing that work.

In 1984 we were planning a nine-city tour of America. At the end of a planning meeting, someone asked, "Would we like P.R. on this tour?" The consensus was, "Yes." Then the tour manager asked, "What kind of P.R. would we like?" and one person said, "Not the kind Shar does."

Whew! I did not know what the person meant and I felt bad but also relieved that I would not have to do the P.R. this time. Then, a couple of weeks later, I was on an airplane headed west toward the first city in advance of the tour. My job? Being in charge of P.R.!

Throughout the flight, I kept thinking, "Not the kind of P.R. Shar does. Not the kind Shar does. What does this mean? What kind do I do?" I really had to think about it. Eventually, after a lot of contemplation and doing the work in many cities, I came to understand. I had viewed P.R. work as endeavoring to "get" something: Get an article, get a cover story, get free publicity, get a public service announcement, get a calendar listing. Get. Get. Get.

It finally dawned on me that "public relations" is a relationship like any other relationship. It will not work if you focus on what you want to get. When we want to get something from people, they feel it and contract.

A good relationship is not only about getting. It is also about giving. It is about offering. We offer our product. We offer our programs to anyone who is interested. We offer information about our courses. We offer volunteers the opportunity to participate.

Whenever my supervisor met with people, at the end she offered them candy. I took that image and began thinking of volunteer work as offering candy to people. If they wanted it, that was splendid. If they did not, that was fine too. It was definitely not the kind of P.R. that I would have done before.

During the next eight years, this wonderful supervisor taught me many valuable secrets about working with volunteers. They were about how to achieve without pulling others down; how to be like the sun which rises every morning flooding the darkness with light without denigrating the night; how we do not have to be angry with the system to uplift it; how, without being gullible, we can be fun-loving and free. In short, they were the secrets by which an organization can be made to flourish.

In ancient times everyone learned from a mentor. Today, it is unusual when someone takes an interest in our growth. If you are one of the fortunate ones who has had a good instructor in volunteer leadership, be grateful. A sage once asked, "What is a human being's greatest support?" The answer was, "Gratitude." So before you begin reading this book, express gratitude for what you have already learned. That will support you in expanding your knowledge.

The next thing to do before proceeding is to take a moment for self-inquiry. Ask yourself, "What is my goal in reading this book?" Be specific. If it is to recruit volunteers, write down a specific number. If it is to attract a definite type of volunteer, write that down. If you are not certain about a goal, ask yourself, "Does my goal meet the organization's needs?"

As you read, always have a pen and notebook close by for jotting down inspirations and for doing the exercises. Write your goal on the first page of the notebook. Many of the ideas suggested in *To Lead Is To Serve* will be new; others will be ideas you are familiar with or have an intuitive knowledge of. Still others will be absolutely known. "Oh, I knew that," you might say. However, knowing and doing are not the same. To attract volunteers and keep them, it is not enough to know how, we have to do it. The exercises are designed to take a good idea, mix it with what you already know and apply it for successful results. As you are reading, when you come to an exercise, stop and do it!

Important: This book is not intended to be implemented all at once. It is designed to be accomplished over one year, one step at a time. Things that arise suddenly, die suddenly, too. Quick changes can quickly dwindle into nothing, so let things evolve.

Go through the book step by step.

Concentrate on one chapter each month and let it permeate the entire organization. It will be easy if you take it a little at a time. When the steps are completed, start over again.

While writing *To Lead Is To Serve: How to Attract Volunteers & Keep Them,* I interviewed 75 leaders who are in charge of many people. They are business executives, volunteer organizers, educators, politicians and religious leaders. Together they have performed more than 1500 years of volunteer service. Their expert advice is incorporated in the thirteen steps and in the appendix. Hopefully, their wisdom and inspiration will serve you.

CHAPTER ONE

To Lead Is To Serve

The first step is to serve.

There is a story in the Talmud about a king and his son. They loved each other very much but they could not get along so the son left home and went far away. After a while, word reached the father that the son was not doing well. The king sent a message to the prince and said, "Come home," but the prince was too proud. He sent a message back to his father, "I cannot."

Then the king sent another message saying, "Just turn around and come as far as you can, and I will meet you wherever you are."

This story expresses the essence of what it means to lead by serving. If we want to lead, we must learn to serve. If we want people to follow us, we have to meet them where they are. Leading them means helping them fulfill their needs.

So often, leaders expect people to be where the leaders are; the same level of commitment, the same level of interest in the project. Sometimes we even expect them to know everything at the beginning. It does not work that way. We have to meet them where they are and lead them to where we want them to go. That is our duty as the person in charge. If we are the leader, we have to be like the king.

To Lead Is To Serve comes from an ancient Chinese teaching. It is in the *I Ching* and the literal translation is, "to rule truly is to serve." The same thing has been said in many ways in many different languages throughout the ages. I think the advice is equally true today.

In any area of our lives, if we want something to happen, we have to serve it. If we want grass to grow, we have to water it. If we want children to learn, we have to educate them. Isn't that the way things work?

Too often, leaders adopt the point of view that because they are in charge, they are supposed to get something from people (time, allegiance, more work.) *To Lead Is To Serve* says when we are in charge, we are the ones who must give.

Once I was working on a large seminar. About 5000 people had come, many more than expected. The ushers became overwhelmed and were not doing a good job of seating people quickly and courteously. They had been trained to treat each person respectfully, but as the crowd grew, they forgot that a "crowd" is still made up of individuals. They began seating them as if they were not people, but a "crowd." My supervisor told me to straighten the ushers out.

We went to a private room and I started pointing out what they were doing wrong and what they should be doing. Later, the supervisor called me and asked, "What did you say to them?" I replied, "I was pointing out how they should have done the seating." She stopped me and inquired, "Did you ask them if they had lunch?"

I was taken aback by her question. However, later I could see that the ushers were under great strain with the big crowds. They needed my support at that time. They needed nourishment from me. They also needed the energy that eating lunch would provide. It was a thoroughly different way of looking at the situation and I have never forgotten the lesson.

People's basic needs must be met before they can accomplish anything. We, the ones in charge, must remember to give basic nourishment. We must look carefully at what people need in order to do a good job and we must serve them in all ways. It was an early lesson for me in *To Lead Is To Serve*.

John Feerick, Dean of Fordham Law School and President of the Association for the Bar of the City of New York, is a tremendous advocate of pro bono (not for fee) legal work. He tells the graduating lawyers, "You have received a lot of schooling, prestige and respect. That makes you part of the aristocracy. You are better off. You must recognize that what goes with that is a responsibility to be helpful to people who have problems dealing with the legal system and the law."

The Upanishads say, "If you want to be happy, be giving." Saint Francis of Assisi said, "It is in giving that we receive." His quote is from a prayer in which he asks,

> *"O Divine Master, grant that I may not so much seek to be consoled, as to console;*
>
> *To be understood, as to understand;*
>
> *To be loved, as to love;*
>
> *For it is in giving that we receive."*

To Lead Is To Serve is a powerful management tool. With little effort, it can make extensive improvements in an organization. An incentive scheme is not a substitute for a really compelling, unifying idea. The motivation arising from a higher idea is the real generator of volunteer commitment.

When it is applied, this principle can create an energetic and loyal volunteer work force, which is priceless. Even on a tight budget, managers can express a sincerely caring attitude.

Application of the *To Lead Is To Serve* principle enables volunteers to achieve beyond the call of duty. It releases creativity and reduces the need for excessive discipline. It allows volunteer organizations to transcend the point at which they are merely surviving.

An organization that serves its volunteers will thrive. Time and money spent on training and supervising volunteers have long range benefits. In fact, every hour spent supervising a volunteer can result in nine hours of volunteer time, according to a cost-benefit study conducted by the State of Hawaii.

A state agency wanted to hire a full-time volunteer coordinator but in order to justify the cost to the Legislature, a study was conducted to determine the value of volunteers. The results showed that, in general, the benefits were at least six times greater than the costs. For a dollar spent on supervising volunteers, six dollars in services were received from them. In terms of time alone, for an hour spent by a staff member in supervision of volunteers, nine hours of volunteer work were received. The study showed that benefits far outweighed the costs, in some cases as much as fourteen to one.

As a result of the study, the state agency now has three paid staff members coordinating the volunteer program.

The principle of *To Lead Is To Serve* applies marvelously to public speaking. No matter what the subject matter, if the speaker holds the thought, "I am here to serve," it wards off fear and frees the communication to come from the heart.

Magic occurs when a speaker shifts the focus off of himself and onto the audience. Stop worrying about, "What are they thinking of me? How am I doing?" Instead, start asking, "What may I do for these people? How can I make them comfortable? By fulfilling their needs, the speech works. Otherwise, it does not.

In every area of life we can ask, "How may I serve?" Consider being in a traffic jam. If we only think, "I've got to get out of this," we get angry and nervous, which causes more of a jam. But if we look at the traffic and say, "Let me serve this situation," invariably something opens up. We see a little space and notice, "If I move over here, then that car can move there," and the problem begins to dissolve.

Jesus taught the lesson of *To Lead Is To Serve*. St. John describes how Jesus, the master, washed the disciples' feet and then said, "If I am your Lord and master, I have given you an example... . If ye know these things, happy are ye that do them."

No matter what we might say aloud, if we are thinking of ourselves and our own needs, that is what we communicate.

Ninety-eight percent of all communication takes place beneath the surface. If we are thinking, "What can I get out of these volunteers?," on a subtle level they feel it and their natural tendency is to put up a defense.

Instead, think, "These people need something. What is it? How can I help?" Invariably, they will feel the support and resistance will give way.

It is a mystical thing, but it works. When the heart is in the right place, whatever we do will succeed.

Once, entertainer Phylicia Rashad was performing her nightclub act in Las Vegas. The act included a 16-piece backup troupe of singers, dancers and band members. It was a fabulous show and completely different from the part she plays on "The Cosby Show." One night, I attended both the early and the late shows.

The next day, Phylicia and I were planning some work we were doing together and we were sitting around the pool talking about *To Lead Is To Serve*. Phylicia really liked the idea.

At the early show that night, she had the audience in her hand. They seemed to want to dance onto the stage with her. The show had been excellent the night before, but this time it was astonishing.

Backstage, I asked Phylicia, "What happened? Why was it so much better tonight?" She said, "I just kept thinking: How can I serve the audience?"

Nothing in the show had changed. She sang the same songs and told the same jokes. It was an inner shift. Instead of trying to demonstrate that she is a good singer and a good dancer, she was thinking, "What can I do for these people? How can I make them happy? How can I serve them?" Instead of thinking about herself, she was thinking about them and it made a magical connection between the performer and the audience. The result was astounding.

Later that night the second show was even better. The band was so alive, it exploded. Afterwards, they came back stage smiling and dancing. Phylicia said this time she had been thinking, "How can I serve the band and the backup singers?"

To Lead Is To Serve. This ancient leadership principle expresses the fundamental idea on which the whole book is based. Phylicia Rashad was successful with it because she understood and applied the principle. You, too, can put the principle to work for your own enduring benefit. To do so is easy. To attract volunteers and keep them, resolve to serve them.

EXERCISE #1

1. Look over your appointments calendar. Before each meeting you plan to attend, ask yourself, "How will I serve this group?"

2. Make a list of three volunteers and ask, "How will I serve these people? What do they need that I can give?"

3. Think of a volunteer who has let you down. What can you do to serve that person?

4. Gradually, step by step, expand the list to include ways to serve all staff and volunteers.

CHAPTER TWO

Be Welcoming

The second step is to be welcoming.

To feel welcome is wonderful, isn't it? On the other hand was there ever a time when you enjoyed feeling unwelcome? Everyone wants to be recognized, greeted and to feel part of the whole. To welcome another human being is a sign of respect and a great service.

In the fourth grade I changed schools in the middle of the spring semester. Neither the new teacher nor the students welcomed me with open arms. I felt like an outsider and changed from someone who loved school to someone who didn't. The result was that my grades plummeted.

It was a relief when the semester came to a close but all summer long I dreaded going back to school. When the first day of class arrived that fall, I was a very timid ten year old opening the classroom door and looking around at a room full of strangers. Then a miracle happened. A little girl smiled and waved and said, "Sit next to me."

Her one gesture of welcome turned everything around for me. School was OK after all.

Welcoming is a powerful tool, yet it is so simple and so obvious that it is often overlooked. Before we can attract new volunteers, we must be able to keep the ones we have by continually making them feel welcome.

Set a Goal
To Welcome Everyone
Who Enters Your Door

At a luncheon sponsored by the Network of Volunteer Leaders, I sat across the table from a man who had conducted a survey to find out why volunteers continue to serve. He queried volunteers at a hospital, a social services organization and a courthouse. The survey concluded that the most significant reason volunteers endured was continuous recognition and appreciation from their immediate supervisors.

The key word is "continuous." Welcoming includes reaching out to people on a regular basis.

Businessman Lex Brodie thinks that non-profit organizations would benefit from treating everyone like a customer. Brodie is a volunteer who serves on the Hawaii Board of Education. After his election, he spent the next ten months visiting every school in the state. There are 239 schools and he sometimes visited a school several times, conversing with teachers, principals, vice principals, staff, students and parents. He said, "In many cases, I was the first member of the Board of Education these educators had ever seen on their campuses."

• To keep volunteers, show interest in them and in their work by making each one feel warmly welcomed on a regular basis.

• To attract volunteers, create a definite plan to make every new person feel welcome and special.

First Impressions Are Lasting

We only have one chance to make a first impression. Keep in mind the saying, "An ounce of prevention is worth a pound of cure." First impressions are lasting, so the way we welcome volunteers the first time will have a long term effect.

Have you ever entered an office, been ignored by the receptionist and then the salesman comes out with a big smile? Everyone deserves a warm greeting the moment they enter the door. If it is the first time, or the tenth, anyone appreciates being welcomed and introduced to others. It is flattering to them and beneficial to us.

Joy Lewis, who is an officer in her political party, says she often discovers the best workers when they are standing alone. "If they have come to an event, it means they are interested but if they don't know anyone, it is hard to get involved."

She recalls,"Once I saw a young

man leaning against a wall at a pot luck. I introduced myself and it turned out he had just moved to this city and was looking for a way to become active. He became very active after that." Joy says, "Someone has to take new people by the hand and introduce them around."

Introducing volunteers to others is an easy way to make them feel wanted. It is hard to be enthusiastic about an organization without a feeling of belonging. Introducing people to others makes them feel part of the group.

A true welcome includes the proper introductions. When introducing two people, apply the principle of *To Lead Is To Serve*. The person making the introductions can serve the people being introduced by giving enough information about each person that a comfortable conversation can ensue. It is not enough to just say the two names and walk away.

Too often, in busy organizations, the one making the introductions hurries through it so he or she can get back to the "real" work. If the goal of the organization is to succeed, making people feel welcome *is* the work.

Respect and kind feelings are always appreciated. It makes no difference how wealthy or how poor or ignorant a person is, everyone is entitled to respect. No matter what the event is, if they receive a warm welcome, volunteers feel infinitely more like coming back again.

A young friend of mine began college recently in her hometown. She had wanted to go away to school, but for financial reasons had to enroll in the local university. She knew many of the students but instead of hanging out with the people she knew from high school, she decided to try to meet people from out of town. She thought this would be more like going away to school.

Every time she saw a student sitting alone she introduced herself. Inevitably, she became the unofficial hostess of the freshman class, making lots of new friends and meeting people from far away. In this way, welcoming others helped her to get over her own disappointment about not going away to school.

It is said that one lake, by itself, gradually dries up; but when two lakes are joined they do not dry up so quickly, because one replenishes the other. It is the same in an organization. People working together can be a refreshing and vitalizing force. Laughter and joy are contagious. Friendly introductions can result in volunteers feeling warm and comfortable with each other.

At special events, officers and board members can make it a point to get around to everyone in attendance to give a warm greeting and say "hello." On an everyday basis, one person can be assigned to do the welcoming. Make a list of staff and regular volunteers for new people to meet. Hosts can find out something about each one, then introduce them to people with similar interests.

Remember to welcome old-timers, too. These are the people who are going to support the organization when the chips are down. Many groups become adept at welcoming new faces, but let their faithful supporters go unnoticed. It is amazing how a warm welcome from the executive director can breathe new life into a seasoned volunteer.

Telephone Smiles

On the telephone, a welcoming attitude can make or break a connection. The person on the telephone is more important than the CEO, because that person is the caller's entire perception of the organization.

Train everyone to have a welcoming attitude on the telephone. To do the training, simply call a meeting of everyone who answers the phone. Ask them to create the guidelines. How do *they* like to be received when they call an organization? How do *they* react when a receptionist is not helpful? How do *they* feel when someone pays attention to them?

A Little Means A Lot

One small expression of welcome can have a long-term benefit. When Jimmy Carter was running for

President, he attended a dinner party in California. The hostess had arranged for guests to change seats after each course so that everyone would have the opportunity to sit next to Carter. It worked out that every guest except one woman sat next to him.

At the end of the evening, the candidate made it a point to speak to this woman, saying, "I'm sorry there wasn't one more course." She said, "At that moment he won my support," and she worked long hours on his campaign.

One quick step to double your chances of success: Be welcoming!

EXERCISE #2

1. How can your organization be more welcoming?

2. Is there a welcome sign on the door or the desk?

3. Do people receive a nice, warm, human smile?

4. *Ask Yourself:*

How can I, in my position, be more welcoming?

When I have felt welcome, what did it?

CHAPTER THREE

Appreciation

The third step is to express appreciation.

Express appreciation often. Develop a system for sending thank you notes immediately and calling volunteers regularly because everyone wants to be appreciated. People volunteer for as many reasons as there are individuals. One way to express appreciation is to find out what each person's special need is.

A few years ago, I went to the dedication of an orchid garden. The speaker was the man who had established the garden. In his talk, he said that when he began the project he did not know anything about orchids.

He told the following story:

Through trial and error he had learned a lot about orchids. He had found that some orchids could be thrown in a corner in a pile of sand and they would grow and bloom and blossom and be beautiful. He really liked these orchids. He did not have to do anything for them.

On the other hand, there were orchids which he had to attend to several times a day. He said he had to mist, fertilize, coax and talk to them in order to get them to grow. But eventually they, too, would bloom and they were beautiful.

When he said that, I thought, "Oh! That's just like people." Some can be told what to do and they do it. They go ahead on their own. While others need so much attention, so much coaxing, so much of our time to tell them what needs to be done. Others need a lot of praise. However, the result is that they all bloom.

Volunteers are rare orchids. Each one needs something different and when we are in charge, we can serve them by giving them what they need. Like the king in the story from the Talmud, we can meet them wherever they are.

Also, when you think about it, the things that are the hardest to grow sometimes end up being the most beautiful (like children), if we are willing to put in our time and effort.

One of the things that often happens in busy organizations is that the leaders get so involved in the work that they forget to do the "watering." This is like the orchid man thinking his job was to bloom and look gorgeous. No! His job was taking care of the orchids so they could bloom.

As the leader, we can be the one who does the planting, watering and background work to help other people bloom. We do not have to worry about blooming ourselves. We can serve by making others look good.

How can we "water" our staff and volunteers? One way is to appreciate them. When an investment appreciates, it goes up in value. It is the same with people. When we appreciate people, they go up in value. Isn't it true?

Tell volunteers that they are appreciated. The New York Philharmonic gives out plaques to do this. The idea is not exceptionally original, but each one is inscribed with a message that is.

Paula Root received a plaque inscribed, *"In grateful recognition of her pioneering, gracious and tireless work on behalf of the New York Philharmonic."* After years of arduous work as a fund-raiser, the plaque is still special to her.

See it as a challenge. Appreciate people by meeting them where they are and discovering what they are good at.

Mary Jane Anaya administers a program selected by the judiciary as a community service center. People who have been convicted can "do time" by doing volunteer work for this program. One young woman, 17 years old, had been arrested three times and was continually truant from school. She had never fit in anywhere, but when she began doing volunteer work she blossomed.

The administrator let the young

woman choose how she wanted to serve. Mary Jane helped her discover what she loves to do, then designed a program to fit this love with the needs of the organization.

The young woman became a "peer director" of five younger children who had similar problems and she chose to teach them kayaking. On the first trip, they ran into rough waters and the girl bravely hooked five boats to her own and pulled them to safety.

This was the first time in her life she had been responsible for anything and probably the first time she had succeeded at something. She was walking on cloud nine.

Next, she planned a three day camp-out where she was in charge of 13 younger children. Previously, this girl had been a straight F student, but to do this, she passed a difficult first aid examination.

This is a beautiful example of *To Lead Is To Serve.* Both the administrator and the young volunteer were leading by serving and everyone benefitted.

Look for ways to help each individual bloom. Every management book says the same thing: People who feel good about themselves do a better job. They take less sick leave. They have more loyalty. They do more creative work. Like watering orchids, we can 'water' volunteers by helping each person feel good about the job that he or she is doing.

There is a coach in Sydney, Australia who knows how to appreciate even the least valuable players. A rugby league team, the Manly Sharks, was fairly second rate when they hired this man as their new coach. One by one he took the younger, weaker players aside and told them, "The other team members have confided to me that they really enjoy having you on the team. They like playing with you."

The result was that over two seasons, the team totally transformed. They rose from the bottom of 25 teams to the top. Also, the players did not trade out to other teams, which is highly unusual. They loyally remained with their team.

EXERCISE #3

1. Name a person who works with you.

2. What do you appreciate about this person?

3. Does he or she need a word of praise? A better piece of equipment? An assistant?

4. How can you help this person progress?

"To everything there is a season and a time for every creature under heaven."

— Ecclesiastes

Give praise at the right time. Undeserved praise backfires and undermines its value. It is said that when someone works for us we should show them our strength first and later show our sweetness. If we show our sweetness first, they'll walk all over us.

Appreciate volunteers when the time is right. Do not procrastinate! When we receive a bill for services rendered, we pay it. We do not like to pay the mortgage late, but we do put off telling someone, "Thank You." Why?

Jo Anne Matchette was a professional fund-raiser for volunteer organizations in Wisconsin for 12 years. She says, "In a dozen years of fund-raising I can count on one hand the gifts that were anonymous. Human beings like to be thanked and recognized."

*"An ounce of mother is
worth a ton of priest."*

– A Spanish Proverb

Making people feel cared for is far
more valuable than telling them your
philosophy. "You have to get on the
phone all the time talking to people,
thanking them," according to Tony
Proffitt, who has been running
successful political campaigns in Texas
for 25 years. He says, "Write regular
thank-you notes. Do not wait until you
need something to contact them."

The president of the Federation of
Jewish Charities, Peggy Tishman,
served on the Wellesley College Board
of Trustees for a dozen years. Although
she is retired from that board now, she
really admires and appreciates
Wellesley for not forgetting about her.
She says, "I'm always invited to events.
Information is always disseminated to
me. It makes an enormous difference.
You never feel, 'Well, now that you've
done your stint they've forgotten you.'"

She also gives Wellesley high marks for doing a super job with acknowledgments. One year the goal was to raise $150 million. They surpassed it, raising $168 million. The college president came to a luncheon at Tavern on the Green in New York City to personally thank everyone who had worked on the project. Peggy says, "Now we can go back to any of those people because the thank you's were done so graciously."

Trust

Another way of appreciating people is to trust them. After we give them something important to do, get out of the way and let them do it.

When he was running for Lt. Governor of Texas, Bob Bullock called together everyone who had ever worked for him, even the ones he had fired. He asked them to support his campaign and told them to do whatever they wanted to do. They named

(CONTINUED AFTER EXERCISE)

EXERCISE #4

1. Write the names of three people you work with.

2. What kind of "water" or "nourishment" does each one need? (E.g., attention, more or less responsibility, instruction, some fun.)

3. Write each name and a type of "water" or "nourishment" on a Post-It. Put it in your calendar for this week.

Erica
Finish the survey she's been waiting for.

Jeena
Tell her that she is needed.

Sam
Visit his office.

4. Make a second copy of each Post-It and put it in your calendar for one month from today.

It is a watchdog reminder. When a month goes by, move the Post-It to the next month. As with orchids, we cannot "water" just once. It needs to be done again and again and again. We know this, but we need to be reminded. That is what the Post-Its do.

themselves the "Bullock Alumni Raiders," placed newspaper ads and had a big, nostalgic party.

Anyone in a leader's position must have the wisdom to attract people who are capable of directing others. This means selecting the right people and then allowing them to have a free hand. If we are too interfering, we will never attract competent people.

It was always difficult for me to trust someone else to do the kind of job I wanted done. The only way I learned was being thrown into a position that was too big for me to single-handedly control. I had no choice but to trust people. And do you know what? They were terrific!

If we let people exercise independent action, they will put forth more effort. When they do, however, we must not disappear into our own project. As the person in charge, we must be there appreciating and reinforcing their efforts.

Strong volunteers need encouragement, too. Supporting strong people brings long-lasting benefits. If the person in charge is wary of strong helpers, the organization will never grow.

One executive director complained that she could not find "good" volunteers. On closer examination, it became apparent that she did not make strong volunteers feel appreciated. She was assuming they could take care of themselves. Also, she was intimidated by the competition. The result was that the organization lost them. Later, when a big project came up there was no one to help.

Appreciating volunteers is like welcoming them; it must be done continuously, like polishing silver.

There is a silver tray in my house that I look at everyday. Occasionally, I get out the silver polish and shine the tray. Then, for awhile, it looks so brilliant that it catches my eye each time I pass by. Inevitably, however, it becomes dull and needs polish again.

I cannot claim credit for putting

the silver in this tray. It was already there. The tray is beautiful on its own, but it doesn't shine unless I do the polishing.

Volunteers are similar to this tray. Like precious metal, they have an inherent value and beauty, but they need to be polished and appreciated again and again.

How do you attract volunteers and keep them? Genuinely and regularly acknowledge, applaud, thank, recognize, relish, admire, esteem, treasure, regard, love, honor, respect and appreciate them.

And Finally

We must learn to appreciate ourselves. We must truly appreciate the great work that we are doing. Do you know what is needed in your organization? You are needed. So never forget how important you are.

Perhaps it is true that in today's world more people are working and fewer are volunteering. Perhaps there are more organizations competing for the same volunteers. But does that make the work we are doing any less valuable? No matter how busy people may be, they are still looking for opportunities to enrich their lives. Volunteer work is priceless. Appreciate what your organization is worth.

If you offered people the Hope Diamond, would they turn it down because they were too busy? Unlikely. Keep this in mind when you offer someone the opportunity to volunteer.

CHAPTER FOUR

Sacrifice

The fourth step is sacrifice.

> *"If you want to be given
> everything, give everything
> up."*

— Lao Tsu

Are you willing to do more than you ask others to do? Are you willing to continue even when your efforts are not appreciated?

The word sacrifice means "to make sacred." People often think of sacrifice as having to give something up, but it is more noble than that. When something is given up, it makes room for something better to evolve.

Parents do this. Their efforts often go unappreciated. They give up a lot, but a human being evolves. They sacrifice themselves, then offer their sacred work to the world in the form of their child.

The entire earth runs on the principle of sacrifice. Everything that is created comes from the sacrifice of something else. The seed sacrifices itself to the soil, the day sacrifices itself to the night, the wood sacrifices itself to the fire.

Have you ever known a company or a project to succeed when there was no sacrifice? To accomplish anything, first we must be willing to give. If we only focus on what we are going to get, nothing will grow. If the seed says, "I'm not going to give myself to the earth," it will never become a gardenia bush.

People who do volunteer work understand this. They do give of themselves and they are making the world sacred.

At the Robert B. McKay Community Outreach Law Program in New York City, many of the volunteer lawyers are sixties activists who went into law to help the world. Along the way, they got caught up with being successful in business. Pro bono volunteer work allows them to do what they originally set out to do.

The Legal Clinic for the Homeless in New York is hot and stuffy and many times the volunteer does a lot of work for a "client" who does not even show up, or a battered woman who goes back to the man, or a drug offender who repeats his crime. The volunteer lawyers have difficulty with this but they continue to serve.

Another example of sacrifice is a woman who has recruited over 100 foster families in the state of Hawaii. She does this by taking the sickest children into her own home. These children are often on a respirator and need constant medical attention. Sometimes they cry continually.

How does she find homes for these children? "God already knows where each child belongs," she says, "We just have to take care of them until the home comes along."

As leaders, we can learn from these volunteers. Like the volunteer lawyers, can we continue to serve even if our efforts are not appreciated? Or, like the foster mother, are we willing to do more than we ask others to do? The more selflessness we adopt in our own work, the more our organization can prosper.

When resources or volunteers are limited, apply restrictions to yourself first. By demanding little of others and still managing to accomplish something, your work will be an inspiration and an example which will attract followers.

When resources and volunteers are abundant, continue to apply restrictions to yourself. People will remember this and when the lean times come again, there will be no resentments.

To Learn About Sacrifice: Study Nature

The sun always rises. Does it ever say, "I've had it"? Never! Does it say, "I worked last week so I'm going to relax?" No. It continues doing its duty. Can we perform our work, our service to the world, as selflessly as the elements perform their work for us?

Can we sacrifice our time? Perhaps we see others struggling to do a job that we have done. In the past, we may have struggled with the same issue or situation. We can take the time to help them. We can offer our expertise in how to make the most of time and resources. We can help them organize their work because we've been through it. People appreciate this.

When volunteers feel burdened or overwhelmed, telling them, "I'll help you," lifts the burden. Often, just the promise that help is on its way is enough to free them from pressure. When the burden is lifted, they often find their own solution.

Everyone wants to feel supported. Letting people express their feelings relieves their pressure and makes things easier. We can give that to them.

Make things physically easier for the volunteers. Take care of their basic needs. If they are working in a room that is too crowded, create a better space. Ask, "Have you had lunch? Are you getting enough exercise? Sleep? Fresh air?"

If they are doing a great job and doing it on an old typewriter, try to get them a computer. Try to help people who work hard by making it easier for them. Through action, let them know they have someone who cares.

Sometimes we have to sacrifice our own popularity. A leader is like the captain on a grand cruise ship. He dresses in his ocean whites and greets people graciously, mingling and chatting like the host at a dinner party. However, when there is a leak in the bow, instantly he is down the hatch plugging the holes or on the deck barking commands.

How many organizations have leaders who only enjoy hosting the dinner party? They love the idea of steering the ship, but in rough waters they run it aground.

Plug the holes. If gossip, unrest and dissatisfaction are springing leaks in the ship, how can the leader best serve? Not by retiring to the stateroom and refusing to become involved.

If gossip is affecting morale, stop it immediately like a captain plugging holes in his ship. Then get the organization back on course by refocusing attention to the original goal.

A leader's strength, knowledge and experience are attributes that can be offered to all. Only those seeds which offer themselves to the earth become trees. Only those leaders who sacrifice themselves become great.

EXERCISE #5

1. Think of a time when someone wanted something from you but you felt like you were too busy. Write down what happened.

2. What could have happened if you had been willing to sacrifice your time to help?

3. Look over a list of people who work with you. Who needs more from you? How can you serve these people?

CHAPTER FIVE
Listen!

The fifth step is to listen.

> *"One way to judge our effectiveness as a leader is the amount of honest feedback that we get."*
>
> — President John F. Kennedy

Leaders tend to be action-oriented, so to stop and listen appears to halt the momentum. But does it? Taking time to listen to people can be our greatest contribution.

People want to be listened to. Isn't this why focus groups are so popular? One organization sent invitations which read, "We want your input so come and help us plan our goals for the next five years." Over 900 people responded!

Listening is a way of showing appreciation and also a way of giving instructions. If you listen to people first, when it is your turn to speak they will be able to hear you.

T.C. Yim was a state senator in Hawaii for many years. Later he was Executive Director of the Office of Hawaiian Affairs. One day an angry staffer came into his office and ranted for over 30 minutes. Without saying a word, Yim just listened. When the man finished, Yim said, "It's noon. Would you like to have lunch?" They finished the conversation over a meal and the man became one of the senator's best employees.

No matter how busy we are, we can find the time to listen. In a crisis, we must make time to listen on the spot. Other times, we can make appointments to listen later.

Before beginning a special project, spending time listening to everyone's ideas will pay off in the long run. This gives the volunteers an investment in the project before it begins. Afterward, listen to people's comments and praise. Honor their good feelings about a job well done by listening to them.

One more good reason to listen: To learn. Sometimes it is difficult to listen to people who do not agree with us or share our point of view, but if we are open to suggestions, the whole organization can benefit.

Sofia Mortada is the Executive Director of the Children's Hope Foundation which helps children with AIDS. The organization is young but is growing quickly. To make sure they are on track, the board of directors meets regularly with volunteers, doctors and social workers to simply ask, "What can we do better?" The organization has prospered from the advice.

Listening Is An Investment

If we do not listen to volunteers, they think we do not value them. We do, so we must find time to listen to them. We cannot expect them to invest energy in our organization if we are not willing to invest our time in them. Listening to people is the

EXERCISE #6

1. Name someone who listens to you attentively.

2. How does it make you feel?

3. What does this person do to listen?

If you had trouble naming someone, it shows how rare good listeners are.

single most important thing we can do to make them feel significant.

When I first became a journalist I was surprised and a bit confused by the number of men whom I interviewed who became infatuated with me. Some professed they were falling in love. It occurred even though these men knew nothing about me and I did not understand why it was happening. Finally, it dawned on me that it was because I was listening to them. All people love it.

To become an effective listener, we have to stop thinking about what we wish to express. How often do we miss what the other person is saying because we are busy planning what we are going to say next?

When a Volunteer Is Upset

Listening is especially important when a volunteer is upset. When something goes wrong, if there is a blow-up or feelings are hurt, it is easy for someone to say, "I'm out of here. I don't need this."

At that moment, remember *To Lead Is To Serve.* Concentrate on understanding how the person feels. Listen for what is really being said. Often it is hurt pride. Even if you think the person is being ridiculous, do not say so; just listen.

When someone is drowning, that is not the time to give swimming instructions. Similarly, when someone's feelings are hurt, that is not the time to teach a lesson. By listening, we can throw a life line.

In the story from the Talmud about the king and his son, if the king had sent a message back to the prince, "You made a big mistake. You should never have left home," do you think the prince would have returned? It seems unlikely.

When someone has totally blown it, that is not the time to offer solutions. No matter how good your advice is, they cannot hear it when they are upset. Hold back and say something sympathetic such as, "I see this meant a lot to you," or "It must feel awful to work so hard and not have it go well."

Holding back is one of the most difficult things for a leader to do. Real leaders can see solutions easily. They see what went wrong and how it could be fixed. However, when someone has blown it, that is not the time to start analyzing. That is the time to exercise patience.

Put your brakes on. According to ancient Chinese wisdom, patience in the highest sense means, "putting brakes on strength." Hold back with your opinion and simply listen.

When volunteers are upset, that is the time to sympathize. Even if they were completely wrong; even if they did it out of anger or stubbornness; to keep an employee, a volunteer, or a friend, listen.

EXERCISE #7

1. Schedule time to make telephone calls to people who have been helpful. You may be on the telephone so much that making another call seems ghastly, but are there volunteers who would love to receive a call from you? Include even the most modest people who faithfully perform the tasks that the organization depends on. Make a list of people to call.

2. Schedule specific times to visit all areas within the organization. Visit every department to listen and give feedback. The department you resist visiting probably needs you the most.

3. Post office hours. Announce, "I am here during this time. Drop in with whatever is on your mind. I want to listen."

CHAPTER SIX

Inspiring, Informative Meetings

The sixth step is to run inspiring, informative meetings.

Inspiring, informative meetings keep volunteers coming back. Boring meetings are probably the number one reason why volunteers resign.

Successful meetings will strengthen the volunteer force and the organization. Meet often, keep meetings brief and be aware that if you talk too much, on a subtle level people begin to dislike you.

How do people feel when we offer them a cup of tea? When we begin to pour it, they feel nourished and grateful toward us, don't they?

What happens if the tea reaches the rim of the cup? Their feelings begin to change and they get anxious. If we continue pouring, the tea spills over the rim into the saucer, then onto their hands, clothes, shoes and the floor. How do they feel about us now?

It is exactly the same when we talk too much. A little is wonderful. A lot is dreadful. Remember: *To Lead Is To Serve*. We want to give information that will serve the volunteers. We do not want to overwhelm them with it.

Use meetings:

- To inspire people
- To follow through
- To inform
- To evaluate current projects
- To train

Do not use meetings to:

- Bore people
- Blame or discourage

Before you begin:

- Set a goal
- Plan the agenda
- Respect time

Set a goal for every meeting, then begin by saying, "The purpose of the meeting is... ."

Almost every person I interviewed for this book commented on the importance of respecting people's time. Start at the appointed hour. Do not go overtime. Do not ramble.

An old saying goes, "When all is said and done, more is said than done." Do not let this happen. The person in charge has to structure the meeting so that no one else has to waste time. People's time is their treasure. We must not squander it.

I served on a committee where the chairwoman opened every weekly meeting with, "OK. What do we have to do this week?" She never took time to prepare an agenda.

It is amazing how many people expect us to spend more of our time listening to them than they have spent to prepare their comments!

Five Keys to Running a Successful Meeting

1. BE INSPIRING

Inspire people by filling them with energy. The word "inspire" means to take an in-breath, which creates energy. We cannot do anything if we cannot breathe. When we fill volunteers with energy, then they can go out and accomplish something.

To inspire others, first we have to inspire ourselves. To be fascinating, we must fascinate ourselves first. Here are some suggestions:

- Share your favorite experiences of volunteering.
- Read a quote giving hope.
- Tell an uplifting story.
- Announce some news that is exciting to the group, e.g., "We just got a big contract or donation," or "A TV station mentioned our project on the news."
- Read a thank you letter.

2. FOLLOW-THROUGH

Briefly mention something from the last meeting and how it has been applied. Following through makes people feel they did not waste their time at the last meeting. A brief follow-through is the key because it reinforces the material without repeating it.

Follow-through is an excellent way to keep the mission of the organization alive in the hearts and minds of volunteers. Successful organizations have clear, understandable mission statements. An important aspect of follow-through is to relate current projects to the overall goals of the organization.

3. INFORM

Give information. Good volunteers like to be informed, especially about their own work. They love statistics about themselves. Announce, "This year we have contacted over 6100 new people; sent out 25,000 pieces of mail; eaten 367 cheese sandwiches, etc."

Use meetings to tell what has

happened and what is coming up. Word of mouth is the most successful form of advertising. Build enthusiasm for a project by announcing, "A great event is taking place."

Public relations expert Dr. Helen Varner says, "An employee on the bus is more important to you than a P.R. person on the evening news. Regularly make sure everyone in the organization knows what is going on."

Inform everyone when the executive director is going to an important conference. This makes individuals feel like they are part of the whole.

One nationwide service organization had an entire department of staff and volunteers quit. Why? Every day the administrator went off to the legislature saying she was going "to lobby." Nothing was explained and they felt left out, so they quit.

People are always striving for union. When they feel included, they give their support. When they feel excluded, they may undermine us.

The Metropolitan Museum of Art in New York City has 1700 employees and

700 volunteers. Vice President of Development Emily Rafferty says, "The volunteers are involved in everything. Giving the volunteers the feeling of belonging is a core function of the museum. They receive the staff newsletter and the volunteer chairperson attends the meetings of the board of trustees."

4. EVALUATE

Take time to evaluate what went right and what went wrong in a project. First, let everyone do it individually. Be quiet and let people write down their concerns, considerations and solutions. Let them share this, then ask:

• How can we improve next time? No matter how good it was, we want to make it better.
• What can we do together to improve?
• What could we do individually?
• What did I learn from the work?
• What will I do differently next time?

It is important for people to write

down or verbalize what they have learned. Everyone remembers what they say more than what you tell them. If they verbalize what they have learned, they will not forget it and they will be stronger for the next project.

The definition of evaluate is "to determine the value of." When we move on to the next project without evaluating the last one, we may not see its value. We may miss out on the gems of what we have accomplished.

We all have great experiences doing volunteer work. Verbalizing them helps us remember. On the other hand, if we have a bad experience, verbalizing it gets it off our chest so we can move on.

Pay attention and learn from these evaluations. If we cannot be influenced ourselves, how can we influence others?

5. TRAINING

In 1993 two women went to work as development directors for two different organizations. Neither woman had done this kind of work before. The first one received extensive training and she was sent to a myriad of seminars. The other was expected to learn on the job. Her organization claimed they did not have funds for "things like seminars." Within three months, donations began flowing in for one organization. Can you guess which one?

Training is worth the investment and volunteers want to receive it so they can do a good job.

Use meetings for in-house training. First do business, then have some kind of training session. Offer something people can really use. The more closely it is tied to a current project, the better.

Have the P.R. person teach volunteers how to write a press release. They will love it and the group may find good writers.

Thirty years ago the aircraft industry began training members of its clerical staff to do a new task called "computer programming." A friend of mine was one of those trainees and today she is considered an expert in the field.

For many people, volunteering leads to successful employment. By offering training, we create a path for volunteers to develop the skills they want and our organization needs.

Most people love training. They feel honored that the organization is willing to invest in them. In this way, it helps them blossom and it helps us find talent.

EXERCISE #8

Plan a meeting according to the steps.

1. What is the purpose of the meeting?

2. How will you inspire people? Which story or quote will you use?

3. On which subjects will you follow-through from the last meeting?

4. What information will you give out?

5. Which projects need to be evaluated?

6. Will you include training?

7. What time will the meeting begin and end?

CHAPTER SEVEN

Be Attractive

The seventh step is to be attractive.

If your organization is having trouble recruiting volunteers, ask yourself, "How am I feeling about my own work? Am I attracted to what I am doing? If not, how will I possibly attract others?" This is not a technique. It is a natural phenomenon.

To attract volunteers, become attractive. Does this mean going to a plastic surgeon for a face lift? No. It is more effortless than that. As an example we can use a coffee cup. When we want to put fresh coffee into a cup, we first pour the old coffee out. When it is full of old coffee grounds, it will not be appetizing nor attractive enough to drink.

To become an attractive organization, clear out negativities. Like washing out the old coffee grounds, we can clear away secret resentments, jealousies or attitudes that interfere with the work and prevent the organization from fulfilling its potential.

A magnet has two poles. The positive side attracts and the negative side repels. A great leader, who is capable of attracting people to a cause, will always identify with the positive.

At the height of World War II, when he was working 18 hours a day, Winston Churchill was asked if he worried about his tremendous responsibilities. He replied, "I am too busy. I have no time for worry."

When we are feeling positive about our work, it attracts others to participate. On the other hand, when we feel overwhelmed or burdened, no one volunteers to join in.

If we are worried about how to "get" volunteers, we can turn the situation around by asking, "What do we need to give?"

There is a businessman in Australia who turned his enterprise around this way. When a recession hit, he found himself facing severe financial difficulties. Not knowing what to do, he went to an advisor and asked for help. He was expecting suggestions such as, "Sell this or that; lay off employees; cut back."

Instead, he was given some interesting advice. He was told, "Treat all of your employees as brothers and sisters. You cannot get your business together externally until you get it together internally."

Based on this recommendation, he changed his focus. Instead of only looking at the bottom line, he started looking at what he could give to his employees. He saw that they needed better working conditions and better benefits. He went through every level of the firm and looked at each person's situation. He asked himself, "How would I treat them if they were my brothers and sisters?"

With this criterion, he made a plan. It would cost money to do the things he needed to do, so he reluctantly sold his beautiful mansion to raise cash.

Then he asked for the support of the employees. He rallied them, saying, "Look, we are in a tough situation," but he tried to save every job. He did everything he could, treating each employee like a brother and sister.

This is a classic example of a leader serving the people who, in turn, gave him their full support. The business turned around and now his products are sold in many parts of the world, including the United States, Hong Kong and Japan. Also, it turned out that he sold his house at the top of the market right before a drop in the price of real estate. Later, he easily bought another.

Cleanliness and Openness Are Attractive

Resources that are not circulated freely tend to congest the whole system. Is there is a computer that only a certain person is allowed to use? Does it create animosity and jealousy? Everything can stagnate from one paltry thing that is hoarded. When resources flow freely, everyone feels they are part of the whole. It changes attitudes and creates a feeling of fresh air within the organization.

EXERCISE #9

In your organization:

1.   Are there ego problems? How could they be resolved?

2.   Are there negative attitudes? How could they be eliminated?

3. How could the leaders communicate more effectively?

To attract volunteers, we can make the office attractive. If it is neat and clean, has flowers and furniture arranged in a nice way, that attractiveness will attract both good volunteers and good ideas.

Jerry Van Camp is a pilot who was the chairman of his pilots' union. The union meetings were held in a room where everyone smoked, ate and drank coffee. Subsequently, it was a mess. At one point in time, the union negotiators had arrived at a deadlock and many meetings had taken place without reaching an agreement. One night, before another meeting, Jerry went into that room and cleaned the whole area himself. He vacuumed, dusted and rearranged the chairs. The chairman became the servant and the next morning the energy in the room and the feelings had changed. Fresh thoughts seemed to spring forth from the fresh atmosphere and the negotiators discovered a perfect solution.

In our homes, if we are going to have guests for dinner, we clean house beforehand. We can do the same thing at the office. To attract good volunteers, the office has to be clean and attractive.

Another law of social physics: When we take good care of what we have, more comes to us.

I knew an industrious woman who worked for a worldwide organization writing its newsletter. She had to travel in her work and for the first two years she used an old, manual typewriter which she set up on her hotel room bed. With no more than that, she put out an excellent newsletter. Of course her talent came to the attention of the company executives. Later, she was promoted again and again and soon she was travelling with a staff and all the computer support that she needed.

Another woman, about the same age and equally as bright, joined the organization at the same time. She made many demands, saying her job could not be done unless she was given better equipment and more help. What do you think happened to that woman? Nothing. Her career came to a screeching halt.

It is a law of nature to fill up things

that are empty and tear down what is full. When the moon is full, it begins to wane and when it is dark, it waxes again. This happens in the lives of people, too. We hate the proud and love the modest. The *I Ching* says, " When a person holds a high position and is nevertheless modest, he shines with the light of wisdom; if he is in a lowly position and is modest, he cannot be passed by."

When we honor what we have, more comes to us. In front of the Plaza Hotel in New York City there is a famous statue which had fallen into disrepair. It was dirty and uncared for. One day, attorney Ira Millstein looked out of his office window across the street and was prompted with an idea. He created what he called the "voluntary window tax." All the offices with windows facing the statue were asked to contribute. They raised $4 million, enough money to fix the statue and put some in trust to keep it clean and in repair. Later, it was learned that the statue is a Greek Goddess and her promise is that when she is treated with respect she will always bless you.

In Oakland, California a neighborhood conducted a clean-up campaign which included planting trees along Stanford Avenue and creating a small park. Later, after all the cleaning up, residents discovered that the neighborhood's crime rate had diminished.

When we take good care of what we have, it will attract more.

EXERCISE #10

1.   Is the office clean?

2.   Without spending money,
how could it become more attractive?

3.   Do people receive a warm,
smiling welcome?

4.   Do you know all of this
already?

5.   Do you do it?

Enthusiasm Is Attractive

There is an elderly Hawaiian woman who has attracted many volunteers for a museum in Honolulu. When I asked where she finds these volunteers, she said, "At the supermarket."

Can you imagine a lady with gray hair wearing a muumuu and flower garland standing in line at the checkout counter asking someone to volunteer? I could not, so I inquired, "The supermarket?" She responded, "Well, the supermarket and everywhere else, too. I just love to volunteer so I can't stop talking about it."

Enthusiasm is extremely attractive. The word *enthusiasm* means "filled with God" and *to attract* means "to offer pleasure and delight." We offer pleasure when we talk about the "sizzle" of our organization.

What do we find wonderful about volunteering? Sharing that with others and infecting them with our enthusiasm is true public relations.

Ancient Secrets of Attraction

The epic poem *The Mahabharata* offers instruction in how to become attractive. A queen asks her Lord, "Who are those beings by whose side you stay and whom you favor?" In part, the Lord responds:

"I always reside with one who is attentive to business, endowed with gratitude and is high-minded in everything. I never reside with one who uses harsh and cruel words, who is distressed at every trifle, and who always indulges in wrath. I never reside with those who think in one strain and act in a different one. I reside with those who observe the virtue of forgiveness, and who are able and prompt in action.

"I reside with those who are devoted to their families and who are properly and neatly attired. I always avoid those who are unclean or impure, who have no patience or fortitude, who are fond of quarreling, and given to much sleep."

Give It Time

After you have given your best efforts to clean up your organization internally and externally, be patient. Sooner or later it *will* attract volunteers. If they do not come immediately, don't worry.

There is a story about a little boy who was walking home from school. On a bush, he saw a butterfly struggling to get out of a cocoon. He watched with fascination and when the struggle continued for awhile he decided to help the butterfly. The boy opened the cocoon and delighted as the butterfly stretched its wings for the very first time.

Then a tragedy occurred. As the butterfly pushed off for its first flight, it plummeted to the ground, dead.

The struggle to get out of the cocoon is exactly what a butterfly needs to make its wings strong enough to fly. If the boy had been willing to wait, the butterfly could have taken flight.

In the same way, if your efforts do not attract volunteers right away, don't feel devastated. Just wait and give it time.

EXERCISE #11

What attracts you? Knowing specifically what attracts you can furnish clues on how to attract volunteers.

1. List five things that have attracted you in your life. It could be a friendly person, a home, Notre Dame Cathedral, etc.

2. What quality made each one appealing? E.g., workmanship, openness, cleanliness.

3. List five ways your organization could become more attractive.

Test question: *How is the Taj Mahal like the Jerry Lewis Telethon?*

Answer: *They were both built from love. They have both lasted.*

CHAPTER EIGHT

Change Your Mind

The eighth step is to change your mind.

The story is told of a woman who thought a beggar had stolen her meal. She was furious with him until he offered to share his cup of tea. Then she thought he was pretty nice. But when her bag of groceries also disappeared, she thought the beggar was a thief. Later, her bag of groceries was found and she thought he was OK after all. Then her meal was found and she felt sheepishly foolish. At last, she found out he was not a beggar; he owned the cafe. She had created the whole thing in her own mind!

The Upanishads say, "As we think, so we become." If we think something is delightful, it becomes delightful. If we think it is going to be overwhelming, it becomes overwhelming.

The mind is analogous to an empty

glass. Whatever we fill it with, that is what it becomes. If we fill it with dirty water, it becomes dirty. If we add salt, it becomes salty. If we pour champagne into the glass, it becomes bubbly. Similarly, if we put a powerful, constructive thought in our mind, that is what we become.

The mind can create any situation. When we are in charge, we have the opportunity to create the situation we desire. We can create an atmosphere that attracts people like bees to honey or we can make them not want to come back again. It is our choice, always.

We can choose to be encouraging. No matter what is going on, we can get in the spirit. We especially need to do this when the outlook is bleak. Any leader can shine when the team is winning. It takes an outstanding leader to inspire volunteers to climb an uphill path.

Abraham Lincoln was a true leader. In the midst of the Civil War he delivered the Gettysburg Address, letting neither death nor hunger sway him from his fundamental beliefs. His faith in what he saw as the highest Truth, inspired such noble words that he was able to stir the deepest feelings in the American people.

Lincoln said, "Four score and seven years ago our fathers brought forth upon this continent, a new nation, conceived in Liberty, and dedicated to the proposition that all men are created equal."

How did Lincoln do this? He was able to change his own mind. He did not let the situation become discouraging. At a very dark time, he applied the principle of *To Lead Is To Serve* and turned to his highest principles to inspire himself and his troops.

Our attitude makes the difference between the group feeling something is going to be difficult or feeling that it will be fun and challenging. How many times have we heard the leader say, "We have so much work and we don't have volunteers. What are we going to do?" If the leader chooses this point of view, how is everyone else going to feel?

This does not mean when we are

feeling discouraged to stand up and say, "Everything is rosy." Never! People know when they are being lied to. When we feel bleak, we can turn to what does inspire us about the work. We can change our own mind before we spread our discouragement to others.

The challenge to the leader is to remain focussed on what is great and inspiring about the project. That is part of the planning process. We can ask ourselves, "Why am I doing this in the first place?"

At any moment the mind can pull us up or take us down. The attitude in the mind of the leader affects the whole group, so we have to be careful.

The same situation can affect two people in completely different ways.

One day Dr. Hal Ferrar was standing in a long line at a bank in Manhattan. He was in a great mood and he was gently whistling a happy tune. Standing in front of him was a lady who was gray all over from her coat to her hat, including a gray cloud of smoke circling above her cigarette.

He continued to whistle when

suddenly the gray lady whirled around and said, "What are you whistling about?" Taken aback, he replied: "I'm just happy I guess." Then the lady asked, "Do you want to know why you are happy?"

"Why?" he inquired and she growled, "Because God is so busy torturing me, He doesn't have time for you!"

"We cook in our own sauce."

– Old Spanish Proverb

Our thoughts really do create our experiences. A little negativity so quickly becomes a demon, a mental monster. On the other hand, if we feel upset or angry, a smile can turn a negative situation around.

I once read a tip for driving that said if you rear-end someone, get out of the car with a big smile on your face. Say, "Gee, I did not mean to do that. I'm very sorry." Keep smiling and it will be very difficult for the other driver to be mad.

I suggested that a friend mention this in a lecture he was giving. He did not want to because he didn't believe it.

The next day he and a passenger were driving down the street. They passed a maternity shop that had a nude, pregnant mannequin in the window. The passenger laughed and said, "Look!" As my friend turned to see it, he rear-ended the car ahead of him. It was a big, shiny black truck. The driver of the truck looked like a body builder as he angrily leapt from behind the wheel.

My friend froze. Then he remembered the story and put on a big smile, saying, "Gee, I didn't mean to do that. I'm very sorry."

The body builder deflated into a couch potato. He said, "OK. Don't do it again," and drove off. My friend happily included the story in his lecture.

> *"Human beings can alter their lives by altering their attitudes of mind."*
>
> – William James

How do we alter our attitudes of mind? How can we change our negative thoughts into positive ones? The most important thing we can do is to step back and watch. Witness our own mind; see how it works, how it chooses the negative or the positive. If we can watch our own thoughts without judging them, great positive growth begins.

Watching without judging is "witnessing." It creates detachment from painful experiences and it is the beginning of freedom from the negative tendencies of the mind.

Zen masters teach the technique of "watching the train go by." We can watch our thoughts just like we watch the cars on a freight train. We can watch them go by but we do not have to jump on.

Play It Again, Sam

In the mind we can always roll a new movie up on the screen and watch the scene play out in a better way. They do this in the movies all the time.

When recording artists do not like the way a certain track sounds, they go

(CONTINUED AFTER EXERCISE #12)

EXERCISE #12

1. Think about a challenging situation by watching all the thoughts you have about it, as if watching a movie. Sit back and roll the thoughts up on the screen in your mind, like rolling the credits at the end of a film. Just watch each thought and then make a list of some of them.

2. Recall an incident that did not go the way you wanted. Recall yourself in the situation.

- *What you said.*
- *What you thought.*
- *What you did.*

3. Now re-write the script. Imagine it differently and improve it.

- *Re-write what you said.*
- *Re-write what you thought.*
- *Re-write what you did.*

4. Watch the re-written scene on the screen in your mind. Play out the new, improved episode in living technicolor.

Test Question:

Did your re-write reflect the attitude of *To Lead Is To Serve*? If not, go back and write it again.

back and record it again. But when we do something we do not like, we think we are stuck with it. Often, we play our mistakes over and over again in our mind.

By repeating the bad scene in our mind, we increase the chances that we'll repeat it again in our life. By changing the scene in our mind, we increase our chances of doing better the next time.

This is especially important when the work has become burdensome. Volunteers often feel overworked. It is not uncommon to hear one say, "When I first became a volunteer, it was so exciting, so rewarding. Then it became work; sometimes even drudgery."

To help a volunteer who feels burdened, have the person go back to the beginning. Ask, "Why did you begin volunteering in the first place? What originally sparked your interest?" Chances are, that spark is still there, smoldering under the pressure. Dig it out and blow a little life into that original impulse.

Before we can help others, however,

we must be sure that we are not feeling burdened ourselves. It is like using an oxygen mask on an airplane. First we must be certain that we can breathe, then we can assist others.

Tom Sawyer's Style

When we are enthused about our work, everyone wants to join in. When we feel burdened, people will disappear. Remember Tom Sawyer painting the fence? When he thought of it as a burdensome chore, no one wanted to help him but when he changed his attitude, acting like his task was his greatest joy, people began begging for a chance to paint.

Holly Henderson, the coordinator of HELP for Non-Profits in Honolulu, Hawaii, counsels that, "When there are not enough resources to go around and the community psyche is depressed, being upbeat instead of tragic is very important."

Holly recommends adopting the Assets Planning Model which looks at what resources an organization has

(CONTINUED AFTER EXERCISE #13)

EXERCISE #13

To rekindle enthusiasm when you feel burdened, first take a few deep breaths, then ask yourself these questions:

1. What did you love about this job at the beginning?

2. What was important about this work?

3. What is challenging about this job now?

4. What is fun about it?

5. What is great or worthwhile about it?

Write these questions on a 3 x 5 card and ask yourself the questions everytime you feel burdened. The answers can rekindle your enthusiasm.

before turning to what it needs. It starts with, "What are the strengths?" instead of, "What is missing?"

It can be applied to individuals as well as organizations. For instance, an employee who has gotten into trouble. Instead of looking for his weaknesses, make a list of his assets: He has a good sense of self-image, he finished school, he has done the job for several years. Use these assets to work with him.

Holly says it is a "very entrepreneurial approach." It is similar to an accountant researching a business to invest in. If it has strong assets, it is a good investment. So are people and programs with strong assets.

She says, "If we focus on need, need, need, we are going to drown in depression. If we focus on strengths and possibilities, we can identify resources we do not usually see and take programs a lot farther than we think."

We will be able to attract many more volunteers by focussing on the positive attributes of our organization.

Holly says, "People will get involved if they think they can make an impact. Be sure to give them a real chance to do that."

Positive Words
Equal
A Positive Response

How we say something can make a formidable difference. The story is told of two high school girls:

One asked the gym teacher: "May I eat ice cream while I begin dieting?"

"Absolutely not!" said the teacher.

The other student then asked, "May I begin dieting while I eat ice cream?"

"Absolutely!"

The response we get depends on how we say things. How does it feel when someone says, "Like it or not, we've got a big job to do?" Doesn't it feel like a big struggle lies ahead? When we hear a comment like this, energy leaves us. We lean back and cross our arms in defense.

However, how do we feel when we hear, "I have some good news?" We sparkle. We lean forward in our chairs. We want to hear it.

How does it sound when someone says, "We have a problem" versus "We have a challenge?"

A positive statement versus a negative one actually physically changes us inside. Human beings are physically attracted to people who use positive words. As the leader, we can serve the organization and the volunteers by changing our negative words into positive ones.

Small Changes
Make A Big Difference

Catherine Kekoa Enomoto is a journalist who tried Exercise #14. She wrote, "I'm overwhelmed by the things on my desk."

When I asked her to write about the work on her desk in a positive way, she laughed and then wrote:

"I love my mail! It gives me ideas. It makes me a better reporter because

I'm on top of the news, and therefore the earlier I get to the mail, the more on top of the news I'll be! March right through that mail!"

Gwen Jackson was the National Chairman of Volunteers for the American Red Cross from 1989 to 1991. When she arrived in Washington, D.C., the first thing she did was change the name on the office door.

From: *Office of the National Chairman of Volunteers*

To: *National Office of Volunteers*

In addition to eliminating the gender, she changed it from her office to their office. This small change marked a tremendous shift in attitude.

Small ways of re-organizing our thinking can make an enormous difference. The more organized our thoughts are, the more we will be perceived as an expert.

Numbering points helps people remember them. For example, "I am going to give you three ideas today," or "This program has six steps."

Gwen Jackson says, "It helps people to remember when you conceptualize your formula." Her formula for volunteerism is:

Three C's & an A
Caring, Committed, Competent & Accountable

EXERCISE #14

1. Re-write these sentences in a positive way:

- It is no use; it's hopeless.
- I've tried, but I just can't do it.
- The tremendous amount of work is overwhelming.
- Almost every time they say, "No."

NOTE: In workshops, there is always a lot of laughter in this section. People enjoy changing things from negative to positive. Even though we are not in a real situation that is truly over-whelming, it is valuable as a practice session. The value is in re-training the mind so that when the real overwhelm comes, we do not succumb to it.

2. Write down a task you face that seems overwhelming.

3. Re-train your mind by writing three positive things about it.

CHAPTER NINE

Have Fun
Everyday

The ninth step is to have fun every day.

> *"The joyous mood is infectious and brings success. Intimidation may achieve something momentarily, but not for all time. On the other hand, when hearts are won by friendliness they will take on all hardships willingly, even death itself, so great is the power of joy over people."*

> — I Ching

The more seriously we take our work, the more important it is to be able to be light-hearted about it. If the *I Ching* is correct in saying people will take on all hardships through joy, then the harder our work is, the more we need to lighten up. When others feel their work is hard, as the leader, we can serve them by sharing our own light-heartedness.

Conductor Zuben Mehta takes the music at the New York Philharmonic very seriously. One day, comedian Danny Kaye asked the maestro if he could conduct the great orchestra. To the surprise of many, Mehta agreed. It was planned as a fund-raiser.

An enormous tent was pitched in Lincoln Center and the comedian was billed as conductor. Some supporters of the orchestra voiced objections, but Mehta's willingness to be light-hearted proved to be remarkably successful.

Danny Kaye led the elated musicians through Beethoven, Sousa and a safety razor commercial! The enraptured audience granted them a standing ovation. Fund-raiser Paula Root says the event grossed $335,000 for the Philharmonic and it broadened the base of the orchestra's supporters.

Humor is a great ally. It can prevent a brilliant leader from becoming arrogant with pride. Pride keeps volunteers away. Humor brings people together.

One year, the partners in a large accounting firm invited the entire office to a luncheon. For entertainment, the senior partners dressed up and put on a fashion show. This was an outright reversal in what was expected from them and people still laugh when they recall the incident.

Laughter is the best medicine for letting go of stress. When we laugh, the whole body relaxes and we feel better physically and emotionally. Anxiety is released and the "big fun" replaces the "big problem."

It is said that if we can look at a difficult person or at someone who really bothers us and laugh at our attitude, then it is divine. If we cannot laugh, then it is our ego and pride. If we take ourselves too seriously, chances are we have a huge ego which will shatter sooner or later. In the meantime, it gets in the way of everything we want to do.

> *"All things come to the person who is modest and kind in a high position."*
>
> – I Ching

Everyone wants to support a leader who is modest and kind, but wants to destroy the person who walks around with his nose up in the air. Isn't it true? It is the nature of the world. High mountains are worn down and valleys are built up. We love the underdog and rip apart the powerful. For example, consider some of the corporate raiders during the 1980's. They made millions of dollars but few Americans were sorry to see them fall. On the other hand, Sam Walton became the richest billionaire in America while still living in his small house and he died in good graces. He remained humble on the ladder to success, so he could climb as high as he wanted to go.

As long as we can laugh at ourselves, we continue to grow. When we start taking ourselves too seriously, we get into trouble.

A dynamic, young businesswoman was highly successful as a volunteer organizer. She lived in the southwest and soon leaders in her community began to talk about a future for her in politics. Newspaper articles were written about her. Then came the fall. Why? A friend said, "She started to believe her own P.R. She became impossible to work with and her future in politics was over before it ever got started."

The *I Ching* says, "If a leader allows himself to be dazzled by fame, he will soon be criticized. If, on the contrary, he remains modest despite his merit, he makes himself beloved and wins the support necessary for carrying his work through to the end."

It is said that if we want to find out about people, give them a little power. Both negative and positive qualities will be revealed.

As our power increases, so must our accountability, responsibility and light-heartedness. When we are in a leadership role, the spotlight is on us. That spotlight brings both our good deeds and our bad deeds into view. Whatever we do is illuminated; it is watched by everyone, so if we become arrogant we bring about our own downfall.

One way to have fun everyday is to let go of extreme ambition, pride and desire. These qualities make us brittle and then we can easily be broken. On the other hand, if we approach our work with joy, we can do our best and stop worrying about the outcome.

I have a friend who is a professional musician. She says when she was a child living in West Virginia she used to sing for hours in the garage, playing her guitar and pretending to entertain audiences. After she became an entertainer by profession, all the fun went out of it. She began to take herself too seriously. She became full of ambition, pride and desire. She was so focussed on fame that she no longer enjoyed the work. After she realized this and let go of it, a lot of the fun came back into her entertaining.

Have fun every day. Nothing attracts like a joyous heart. It is said,

"Everybody loves a lover." People want to participate when we are loving what we are doing and focussing on the fun. They want to help. They respond from far, far away. On the other hand, if we are focussed on how hard a project is, how much work there is and how few people there are to do it, does anyone show up? Never! They run the opposite way.

I used to notice on days when I felt lonely and tried to call a friend, nobody was home. On days when I was full of enthusiasm and energy, my phone rang all day long with invitations. It is energy. What we put out is what comes back to us.

We can serve our organization by putting out joyous energy. This is especially true when we have made a mistake. When we can admit our mistakes and be light-hearted about them, we grow. It frees us to move on. Otherwise we get stuck defending our position because the ego will do anything to justify itself.

You may ask, "What if the situation is not funny? What if it is horrendous?"

Have you ever noticed how the funniest movies are based on absolutely horrible situations?

"Sister Act," a film starring Whoopi Goldberg, is about a nightclub singer who unwillingly winds up in a convent. Taken seriously, it would be a horrible situation both for the singer and for the nuns. Can you imagine how the mother superior would cope with it? However, as a comedy, it is just this intensity and friction that make the movie so funny.

To serve volunteers, let our lives express the comic side of intense situations. After all, what do we have to lose?

Catastrophic moments are so much fun to laugh about later. When we stop fighting the events in our lives, we get more than we had planned for. When we let our solutions go, we begin to grow. When we laugh at ourselves, we begin to get a taste of true living, true leadership and that great force called "life's flow." Go with the flow. Laugh with the lot. When we stop fighting our situation, we have a lot more fun.

The funniest moments are often

human events occurring exactly as they do. We do not have to tell jokes to be funny. We can simply notice the way things are.

In *Crazy English*, author Richard Lederer does this with the English language in an exceptionally amusing way. He probes, "How can a slim chance and a fat chance be the same, while a wise man and a wise guy are opposites? How can the weather be hot as hell one day and cold as hell the next? You have to marvel at the unique lunacy of a language in which your house can burn up as it burns down, in which you fill in a form by filling it out and in which your alarm clock goes off by going on."

Lederer points out how things are and it is delightfully funny. We can too.

EXERCISE #15

1. Have fun today.

2. Do it again tomorrow.

CHAPTER TEN

Be Creative

The tenth step is to be creative.

Creative ideas attract creative people. Creative organizations attract creative volunteers.

One definition for the word "create" is "to invest with a new form." No matter how great the Carousel Ball was last year and the year before that, has it become merely another Carousel Ball? Does the project need to take on a new form? Creating new vehicles for volunteers will keep them inspired.

Are you looking for a way to keep volunteers committed? Use your creativity. Earl Yonehara was searching for a way to do this at the Hawaii State Judiciary and came up with the idea of offering volunteers a judicial appointment. He had official appointment forms drawn up on old parchment paper. First, the volunteers attend a training program and then they attend a swearing-in ceremony with the Chief Justice of the State Supreme Court. They take an oath to "solemnly swear that they will faithfully discharge their duties as a citizen volunteer." After that they receive a judicial appointment committing their service for a certain number of months or one year.

Earl says involving a top administrator (in his case, the Chief Justice) sends a message to the paid staff that the volunteers are important. Also, the definite time commitment makes it easier for the staff to invest time in training volunteers.

Look for creative ways to accomplish your goals and include volunteers in the creative process. This keeps them interested and helps the organization to remain dynamic.

How Does an Organization Become Creative?

I once had a job in which I had to come up with a new idea every day. At first I thought, "This is impossible. How can I come up with something new every day?" I worried about it a lot. Then one day it dawned on me that God comes up with a new day every day. God creates every face differently, every snowflake unique and every moment unlike the last. If we are created in God's image, then we must have some of that creative ability, too.

After that insight, I changed. I did not magically come up with a new idea every day, but I no longer thought it was impossible. I knew it was possible.

The Kashmir Shaivism theory of aesthetics says that creativity is born out of stillness. Kashmir lies in the foothills of the Himalayas. Shaivism is a philosophy based on the oneness of all things. The theory says that the initial creative impulse is a flash of awareness. Later, this awareness takes form. When it comes to a painter, it is in the form of a painting; a sculptor sees a statue; an economist a new theory; an organizer a new format, and so on.

The creation is born complete. Michelangelo expressed his experience of this, saying when he looked at a piece of marble he saw the form finished and all he had to do was peel it away.

Artist Dan Warner says he sometimes just sits and looks at a blank canvas for hours before he feels like doing something. Other times, he pushes himself to start painting. He works on it and works on it until finally something starts to happen.

He says, "Then, magic arises and you are in a different state. You are full of enthusiasm and you do not want to go home. When this happens you are painting automatically and it is so easy. But up to that point, it is so laborious and difficult. The magic does not happen with every painting, but when it does the result is something that I am really pleased with. I don't know what makes it happen. It is hard to say. A really nice feeling arises and you feel still."

So, to get started with creativity, just get started.

Ria Keltz-Remenar, an artist who is also a realtor told us, "I learned from real estate that when nothing is happening, just do something. It doesn't really matter what I do, as long as I do something. Any action will cause a reaction. I applied it to my art and it gets me going every time. Just do something."

Another artist, who designs window displays at a department store, says when she first got her job, every time she changed a mannequin the dress would sell. Then she would have to change the display again. She got tired of changing the display, so she started using dresses that she did not think would sell. No luck! Eventually she realized it had nothing to do with the dress, but merely taking action.

She says it is the same with her art. If she just does something (even clean the brushes) then the energy begins to flow. It is like breathing life into the project and something else takes over.

"If you have a blank canvas, you have to put something on it," says Dan Warner, "and once you put something on it, then you have broken the spell. You have made the commitment. It's not the commitment, though, it's the first action. Taking that first step is what does it."

In the Kashmir Shaivism theory of aesthetics, it is said that a complete aesthetic experience is made up of nine "rasas." The word is translated "juice" or "nectar." In a loose sense, it could be called the nine flavors. These are: Odious, terrible, erotic, heroic, comic, pathetic, furious, marvelous and serene. Art has to have all of these woven together to create a complete aesthetic experience.

Creative Leadership

So, how does all of this apply to being in charge of volunteers? It suggests a form of leadership. Do not get stuck in one style. Do not get stuck in terrible when you could easily be serene; or comic when you should be forceful.

Use your creativity to find the right job for each person, even the most difficult one. In the hands of a great master, everything is of value. An artist has a lot of colors on the palette and an organization has a lot of different kinds of people. Like a good artist, the creative volunteer leader makes the best use of each one.

Be creative in the projects that you plan. Make some small and others enormous; some simple and some strenuous.

When making up a team to work together, the event will be more interesting if there are different flavors of people. Think of it as cooking. You would never plan a menu of all potatoes. Do not plan a committee of potatoes, either.

A master chef will balance a meal to include the five tastes: Sweet, sour, salty, bitter and pungent. When we look at a project in this way, we see the value of having different kinds of people in the group. We may not like someone who is sour, but that person might be exactly what is required to balance the committee.

Successful creativity includes being creative with the resources that we have. Aren't the best cooks the ones who can go into the kitchen and whip up something with whatever is available?

Perhaps you say you are not that kind of cook? You might not think you are creative, but you do have setbacks, don't you?

Creative Solutions

The greatest creativity is often borne from misfortune. Hemingway wrote about his anguish. Bill Cosby creates comedy out of adversity. Many of the most creative ideas on earth have come from a calamity. Every great product is created in answer to a need and many, many noteworthy volunteer projects have been born from suffering.

Use setbacks to become creative. This is what management books refer to as being "proactive."

Dr. Sharon Miyashiro was organizing a women's rally for a senatorial candidate, but interest was low. A few days before the event, it seemed like the rally would be a big dud.

Then a florist friend called and said someone had cancelled an order for 2500 roses. Could Sharon think of any use for them?

She spent a few quiet moments thinking about how to use the roses. Her best memory was receiving one, which gave her an idea. She had to act quickly so she called on people who had helped her before. She telephoned six volunteers and sincerely said, "I need your help."

Sharon says, "They responded because it was a good cause and also because people want to be asked." The six were able to swiftly mobilize 30 volunteers. They came together to de-thorn each rose and printed small tags announcing the women's rally which were attached with a yellow ribbon. At lunchtime, they went downtown and stood on the five busiest street corners passing out the roses.

Everyone wanted one. Secretaries were leaning out of office windows calling, "Save one for me!" A TV crew videotaped the rush for the roses. A newspaper printed a photo.

The event went from a non-event to a grand success and many at the rally said they came because of the roses. Sharon said the 30 volunteers came right back asking, "What's next?" She says, "Letting people get a taste of success at an easy task is a terrific formula for future success."

Realtor Barbara Dew has been a volunteer for many organizations. She shared information that she had been given that a severe drop in membership was the catalyst for creative change in the Girl Scout organization. The leadership went to Harvard Business School and asked for advice. They queried, "If we were a company losing clients, what would you recommend?"

The Girl Scouts received some interesting counsel: Even if you are a volunteer organization, you must run it like a business. Divide the leadership into someone who takes care of the nuts and bolts of managing and an executive who is a public relations person for the organization. This executive should spend a lot of time at social events representing the Girl Scouts.

They were told to broaden their base and keep up with the times, so as not to lose steam. The Girl Scouts began

"Space Camps" and programs that were entirely modern. They also started using nostalgia in their promotions. At large events, they would announce, "If there is anyone here who was ever a Girl Scout, please stand up." Many women would stand, reminding each one of a fond memory and this rekindled enthusiasm for Scouting.

In this case, the drop in membership created a wonderful opportunity for regeneration. The Girl Scout organization used its problems to launch some dynamic new programs.

To find creative solutions, take a good look at what your organization has a lot of and what it has too little of.

The Pennfield School in Wisconsin serves children with disabilities. They were having a capital fund drive and wanted to recruit celebrity help when an advertising agency suggested they recruit some politicians.

The State of Wisconsin had eight living ex-governors. All eight were recruited and the event included a tour of the school by the governors. They made a video showing them watching the children succeed in accomplishing small, difficult tasks. When the video was shown at the luncheon, there were few dry eyes in the crowd. One governor said, "I want to thank the women's movement for making it OK to cry at lunch today."

Enough money was raised to build a new wing onto the school and it is called, "The Governors' Wing."

EXERCISE #16

1. List five things your organization has a lot of.

2. List five things your organization would like more of.

3. Ask people to find solutions to #2 in list #1. For example:

- Low interest in the rally and a lot of roses
- Few new Girl Scouts and many former members
- Needing a celebrity sponsor and having eight ex-governors

Approach it like a game. Let children help. They are great at it.

CHAPTER ELEVEN

Teams That Work

The eleventh step is to create teams that work.

People feel happiest when they feel they belong. A dynamic organization is like a beautiful bracelet. Each jewel in the bracelet may be exquisite, but the strength lies in the connection. A pile of loose, individual gems is actually more of a nuisance than anything else.

Constantly look for ways to make the volunteers feel connected. Almost any group can accomplish more than an individual. When team work is strong, good ideas will bubble up to the surface so the challenge to the leader is connecting individuals into a solid team. The stronger that connection is, the more powerful the group will be.

An Air Force officer told me how he begins building strong teams from the first day of orientation. On a blackboard he draws a diagram of all the jobs on the base. Every position is marked with an X. Then he points out where each person fits in, telling them, "See that X there? That is you and your X is just as big as the Commander's X. If you don't do your job, the Commander can't do his."

The officer says a lot of new recruits to the Air Force do not consider their job to be important unless they are pilots. To them he says, "Your job makes it possible for others to do what they have to do. Every job is essential. For instance, if you are in Finance, a pilot can't fly without you. You make sure his family gets a monthly check so when you do your job it eases his mind. If he had to worry, how could he concentrate on flying?"

Individual Work Is Weak Team Work Is Strong

A dramatic example of the benefits of strong team work to a volunteer organization was illustrated by a social worker, Sue King, who volunteered to organize the refreshments for her meditation organization. Under the previous refreshment chairperson, almost no one volunteered to help and the refreshments were a disaster. Within two weeks, Sue King had 48 people helping.

This is how she recruited so many volunteers:

There were eight programs per month and her task was to recruit six people to donate refreshments for each program. She needed 48 people per month.

The previous chairperson became completely overwhelmed trying to recruit that many volunteers. Eventually she gave up recruiting and tried to bake most of the refreshments herself. This was a huge task so she became overwrought and burned out.

Sue King quickly devised a better plan. She made eight lists, one for each program. At the top of every list she wrote "Team Captain." Then she wrote "Numbers 1-6."

Team
Captain:_____

1. _____
2. _____
3. _____
4. _____
5. _____
6. _____

Instead of recruiting all 48 people herself, she recruited eight team captains who were willing to be in charge once a month. They each recruited six people who would donate one refreshment a month. When the first woman was in charge, she and a couple of other people were begrudgingly doing everything. Under this plan, more than 48 people were happily participating.

One of the secrets to this design's success is that Sue King continually served the team captains. She applied the principle of *To Lead Is To Serve* and if a captain could not find six people, she helped recruit. Since she was not baking everything herself, she had time to meet people and ask if they would like to participate. She constantly made the team captains feel that she was supporting them.

Another secret to the plan's success is dividing the work into small increments. The first woman was trying to recruit 48 people. Sue was only looking for eight.

In the Bible, Nehemiah rebuilt the wall of Jerusalem in the same way. It was such a big task that most people thought it could not be done. However, with each person being responsible for a small portion, a huge mission was accomplished very quickly. The Bible describes in detail how each group rebuilt its own small section of the wall. While reading this, I could envision each group doing its part with great enthusiasm. It reminded me of volunteer projects. They are always more successful when a lot of people do a little, as opposed to one or two people doing everything.

"The journey of 1000 miles begins with a single step."

– Lao Tsu

Any project that seems big and overwhelming can be approached in this way: Little by little by little. Divide the work into small steps.

While writing this book, at one point the computer seemed to collapse. It became slower and slower and slower. I was almost at the end of the project and did not want the computer to completely quit so I went out and bought a new one only to discover the new computer was almost as slow. I did not understand what was going wrong.

Then someone advised me to divide the book into groups of chapters and let the computer handle a few at a time. After I divided the work into small increments, the computer came right up to speed. In the same way, when we are working on any large project, it will be a great deal easier if we divide it into small steps.

EXERCISE #17

1. Write down a sizable task that you face.

2. Name three to eight people who could be "team captains" on this task.

3. What would each team captain be expected to do?

4. How many people would each captain need to recruit?

5. What would each person be expected to do? E.g., Bake a refreshment once a month.

Where There Is Friction, There Is Weakness

Where there is friction between two links of a bracelet, that is where it will break. This is also true on a team and on a committee. Where there is friction between people, the work becomes weak.

Find the weak links and strengthen them. Assist the parts to cooperate for the benefit of the whole. Sometimes all it takes is asking people to sit down and talk. When they do, the friction often develops into a source of tremendous creativity. Good communication makes an enormous difference in a team effort.

Communicating Means Winning

"Communicating means winning" was the finding of an 18-month study by Dr. Jim Loehr of *Tennis Magazine*. Dr. Loehr says, "Talk is an extremely valuable way to improve your team's winning percentage."

In his study of amateur, college and professional tennis doubles teams, the results were astonishing: At the pro level, partners talked between 83 percent of the points. The best college teams came together between 69 percent of the points.

But the amateur teams? They only talked between 17 percent of the points. In fact, amateurs communicated more to the opponents than with their partners!

The study reveals that the more professional a team is, the more it communicates. Dr. Loehr says, "Simply put, if you want to win, talk. It's especially important during the bad times. Great teams face adversity together, not individually."

One year there were two tennis teams at Punahou School in Honolulu. There was a gold team and a blue team. The gold team was made up of the superstar tennis players. They were students who had taken lessons all their lives. They had the latest equipment and great outfits. Individually, each member had beautiful strokes.

The blue team was made up of the students who enjoyed the game, but it was a side event for them. They were enthusiastic about tennis, but they had not devoted a lot of time to it. They did not have the skills nor the elaborate equipment that the gold team had.

As the semester progressed, the coach noticed that during the tournaments the blue team members always stayed to cheer on their teammates. The gold team members would leave as soon as their individual matches were over while the blue team members, even if they were losing their matches, would bring snacks and water and stay to encourage their teammates until the very last point was played.

In the middle of the semester something turned around and in the end the blue team actually beat the gold team. The coach said as individuals they were not the top players, but team work made it possible for them to take the trophy.

Planning for adversity will help build strong teams. Once adversity is upon us, it is too late to call time-out and agree on how to handle it. But we can plan ahead. Dr. Loehr recommends five questions to ask your tennis partner about adverse situations before the situation arises.

We used the questions with workers in a volunteer agency that was undergoing a considerable personnel turnover. The exercise told the group a lot about each other. It also strengthened the links that tied the team together.

HOW CAN I HELP?

1. How can I help when you're nervous?

2. How should I react after you've made a dumb mistake?

3. How should I respond when you lose your temper?

4. How can I help when you're playing terribly (doing a bad job)?

5. How can I help when you're getting down on yourself?

Each person wrote answers to the questions. Then we went around the group and everyone reported aloud his or her answers. (If the team is large, divide into smaller groups of people who work closely together.)

On Question #5, a woman said that when she got down on herself she wanted the others to tell her to throw that attitude out the window and move on. Within one hour, in another discussion, she got down on herself. Two people in the group remembered her wish and said laughingly, "Throw it out the window and move on!" She hesitated for an instant, then joined in the laughter and moved on.

A note about this exercise: It brings out people's goodness. It makes everyone want to help each other. It also reveals that when we are not doing our best, we want other people's understanding and support instead of criticism. Not one person said that they could be helped by the others telling them what they had done wrong.

EXERCISE #18

Sit down with one of your teams and go through the five questions on page 171, "How Can I Help?"

CHAPTER TWELVE

Letting Go

The twelfth step is letting go.

Sometimes the best way we can serve volunteers is to let go of them. I used to have a volunteer assistant whom I relied on tremendously. She was dependable, organized and loyal. However, this assistant was not blossoming in her position. She was qualified to handle more responsibility but because I felt so dependent on the support that she gave me, I was not thinking of her growth. I was not serving her.

More than once my supervisor hinted that she should move on but I could not let her go. I depended on her too much. Finally, my supervisor offered her a better position.

When she left the office, another volunteer replaced her. This man was also dependable, organized and loyal. In addition, he was tremendously creative. With his help, our work flourished and the department grew. The woman who had left did, too. She went on to a position in which she was able to shine.

When it is time to let go, it is time to let go. I was so afraid of losing the support my assistant gave that I failed to see how tightly I was holding on to her.

Let Whoever Comes, Come and Whoever Goes, Go

Do not hold on to people too tightly. A story is told of two couples who were walking on the beach when the younger woman asked, "How did you stay married for 40 years?"

The older woman did not respond immediately. Eventually, she reached down and picked up some sand. As she squeezed it tightly, sand flowed out between her fingers and when she opened her fist, only half of the grains remained.

"When you hold on too tightly, you lose it," she said. Then she picked up more sand and gently cradled it, open fisted. She held it very loosely and every grain stayed in her hand.

Have you squeezed volunteers like this? Or do you cradle them loosely? Clinging to volunteers too tightly will scare them away.

It is said that if something truly belongs to us it cannot be lost, even if we throw it away. So do not worry.

Welcome people and let them know they are appreciated; listen to them and offer challenging, creative volunteer projects. If they do not thrive, then let them go.

When an orchid is in its proper soil, it will bloom. If it is not, no matter how much attention it receives, it will not flourish.

Let go of using guilt as a motivator. Guilt creates stagnation. It is like a gardener pouring poison on the plants. Guilt kills energy and enthusiasm for the work, so never make anyone feel guilty.

If volunteers are doing the work out of guilt, how effective can they be? A poisoned plant cannot bloom. When we let go of guilt, it leaves more room for enthusiasm.

Letting people move around within the organization will help you keep good volunteers. People who like each other tend to work well together and cooperate. If leaders recognize this, the organization will profit from a sense of trust.

Letting a Volunteer Go

What happens when volunteers do not want to leave but we want to let them go?

To let go of troublesome volunteers, Mary Jane Anaya of the Kauai Non-Profit Resource Center says she has had great luck with the advice of the *One Minute Manager*. She begins by asking the person, "Do you feel you are doing the very best that you can in this position?" She says no one ever answers, "Yes." They know they are not doing well, even if at first they do not feel safe to admit it.

Then Mary Jane asks, "What do you think we ought to do about it?"

She says, "They fire themselves. Usually they say, 'I should not be in this position. I really do not like this kind of work. I thought I would, but I do not.'"

She advises that when an employee or a volunteer departs, "Do not talk stink behind anyone's back. It always gets back to them. Let them leave with complete dignity and self-esteem. Then they have something good to say about your organization."

Appreciate them. Thank them. If you let people leave with dignity, they can learn from the experience. If they put a lot of energy into defending their self-worth, there will not be energy left over for changing.

To discipline people or let them go, take someone else along. Then there is a collaborator to offer a different perspective and lend support. No matter how experienced we are, it can be difficult to give out bad news.

On the other hand, if we are losing employees or volunteers, we can ask collaborators to point out what we are doing to create this. When a plant begins dying, gardeners have to look at the fertilizer they are using and the water, air and soil. If several plants die, something is wrong.

When several volunteers leave, something is definitely wrong. Do not play ostrich. Ask for honest feedback from those who are leaving. Set aside pride and sincerely question, "What do we need to change?" This can benefit the volunteers, the leaders and the organization.

After Letting Go

Volunteer work can soothe the soul. Gossip and office politics are the last things a volunteer organization needs.

Forgive and forget. Clear the air and move on. As soon as you do, the organization will begin to feel more healthy and functional.

EXERCISE #19

1. What am I creating in this organization which is not beneficial?

2. Do I let people do what they do best?

3. How do I react when volunteers do not follow-through?

4. Do I make people feel guilty?

5. What will I do to change?

CHAPTER THIRTEEN

Reaching Our Goals

The final step is to reach our goals.

*"The moment one definitely
commits oneself,
then Providence moves too."*

– Goethe

By now you may be saying, "I have tried all of these things.   I believe in this. I am like the king in the Talmud. I meet people halfway, but it does not always work. Too many things get in the way."

My response is, "How do you think Edison felt?" Thomas Edison tried 10,000 times to invent the light bulb. When asked, "How did it feel to fail 10,000 times?" he replied, "I did not fail. I learned 10,000 ways it would not work."

Edison refused to call it 10,000

"failures." He saw it as 10,000 lessons learned. How many "lessons" will we learn? There must be a principle of social physics that goes like this: "The degree of success is proportional to the number of obstacles overcome."

Gold becomes pure by being subjected to fire. A muscle gets strong from repeated resistance. In the same way, people and projects succeed after repeated trials and errors.

You Cannot Fail

Many years ago I was an entertainment reporter in Hollywood. The awards shows always gave recognition to the "Best New Artist," "Best New Group," etc. I would often interview the "Best New Star" only to find out he or she had been in the business for 10 or 15 years! The "new success" came after years of what some would call failures. We will call them "lessons."

These creative artists had learned another principle of social physics: You cannot fail unless you quit.

Why would we quit? Fear. Fear

stops us. Fear of what people think. Fear of whether or not we can accomplish it. Will I succeed? Will I look foolish? Am I capable of doing this? Have I taken on more than I can handle? Is it worth it?

Fear causes paralysis. Look at what happens to our bodies when we become afraid. We stop breathing, muscles tighten, everything stops circulating.

Once I was skiing in Sun Valley, Idaho, and found myself in a class that was much more daring than I was ready for. Most of the time we were on steep slopes that scared me to death. However, we had a great instructor who told us something I will never forget. He said, "Keep your eyes on the distance. Look at the skyline and the beautiful mountains. Keep looking ahead. When you see yourself as part of the big picture, everything appears to be moving very slowly. On the other hand, if you look down at your feet, you seem to be moving so fast you are out of control."

When you get scared: Keep your eyes on the big picture.

To Hit the Target, Constantly Keep the Goal In Sight

"If the trumpet does not sound a clear call, who will get ready for battle?"

– Corinthians

To accomplish anything, we must constantly keep the goal in sight. This makes it more likely that we will reach it and also makes it easier to attract volunteers to help us.

In sports, more spectators attend the games in which they can see the goal line, such as football, soccer and horse racing. Fewer people go to watch long distance running.

As the leader, we can serve volunteers by helping them keep the goal in sight at all times. Never let them forget why they are volunteering. Constantly cheer them on toward the goal line and gently correct them when they get off course, reminding them which direction we are going.

Many things come up in every organization including complicated relationships, pride and power struggles. These are like the bumps and setbacks that football players experience along the field. But when the running back crosses the goal line with 80,000 people cheering, all those bangs become well worth the effort and the player usually cannot wait to get back out on the field.

It is the same with volunteers. We can help them go through the bumps and bangs of volunteering by making the goal line very clear and continually pointing them toward it.

To Reach A Goal

A study was done of Harvard graduates. A decade after graduation, the alumni were asked about their accomplishments. The study found that the ones who had a goal in mind at graduation time had been three times more successful than the ones who had no goal. The ones who had a goal and had written that goal down had been 10 times more successful!

In one of our workshops on "How to Attract Volunteers & Keep Them," we had just introduced this information about writing down your goal when a participant raised her hand and asked if she could say something to the group. She was from a local chapter of the American Diabetes Association where we had given the workshop a year earlier. She shared that previously the most money her organization had raised in one year was $70,000. After the workshop, they met and set a goal for $100,000 and wrote the goal down. That year they raised $121,000!

Set a Goal

When we set a goal, it elicits others to support us. The New York Philharmonic had a three-day radiothon. For 72 hours they continually announced the goal over the radio. As it neared the end and the goal had not been reached, public support began to roll in. Even a cab driver called in with a pledge saying, "You've got to meet that goal or I'm gonna give you all my tips!"

Spectators love to cheer at the finish line. People's good wishes help an athlete and they help an organization. Why do people love to play games? Games have clearly defined goals which bring a lot of pleasure to the human species. When we set a clear goal, it makes people very happy when we realize it. It also inspires people to give their time, money and good feelings to help us reach it.

When volunteers are working alone, a clear goal will help them remain committed. Let them know, "We need 95 envelopes addressed," or, "We must call 25 members today."

There is a certain type of volunteer who cannot quit until the project is completed. A clearly defined, achievable goal will keep that person working until the very end.

By the way, the Philharmonic did meet that goal!

Write The Goal Down

Putting a goal in writing makes it easier to achieve. Post the goal and keep it right in front of you at all times. If it is sitting on your desk staring you in the eye when the phone rings with an interesting diversion, looking at the goal makes it easier to say, "Not now." Looking at the written goal when you are planning the day or the week helps, too. What percentage of time are you investing in what you truly wish to achieve?

Make A Plan

Make a specific plan for reaching the goal. It is like using a road map. By following a map, the chances of reaching a chosen destination are infinitely greater than only a vague notion of the direction. Even a crude map is better than none. Even a crude plan for reaching a goal will be more successful than no plan.

Don't forget: It is in giving that we receive. What amount of time and effort are you willing to give in exchange for achieving the goal? What quality of work will you do? This needs to be included in the plan.

EXERCISE #20

1. Write down a long term goal.

2. Make a list of reasons why achieving this goal will benefit you and others. Make them convincing enough to convince yourself.

3. Make a plan. What will you do to reach this goal?

4. Post your personal goals in a place where you can see them every day. Post the goals of the organization in a place where everyone can see them. This is essential.

5. What step will you take today toward reaching the goal? A great river begins with a drop of water. Even the most enormous projects begin with one small step.

"The best remedy for those who are afraid, lonely or unhappy is to go outside, somewhere where they can be quite alone with the heavens, nature and God. I firmly believe that nature brings solace in all troubles."

– Anne Frank
The Diary of a Young Girl

A Technique
for Reaching Our Goals

Before beginning the technique, we must understand an important point about obstacles: They are there for a reason. Behind every obstruction is a great opening, a great opportunity. Obstacles are there to teach us something, to change our direction, to hold us back for awhile until the time is right, even to protect us.

A very successful developer was planning to build 125 condominiums on the Hawaiian island of Kauai. He had bought the property, hired a contractor and was ready to go. However, he could not get a permit. For three years he could not get a permit.

The housing was needed. Kauai had a shortage. These condos were modestly priced. They were environmentally planned. Still, he could not get the permit.

Then a hurricane hit Kauai. Fifty per cent of the buildings on the island were damaged or destroyed. Since he had not gotten the permit, his had never been built. What he thought was an obstacle, protected him.

In Nagasaki, Japan there is a mountain lookout for tourists. From this point, it is possible to see the entire section of the city that was destroyed by the atomic bomb. The guide explains that the only people who survived the attack lived on the other side of the mountain. When I heard this I could not help thinking that before the bomb, the mountain must have been very difficult to cross whenever one wanted to go into the city or down to the shore. Those residents probably saw the mountain as a huge obstacle. Instead, it saved their lives.

This is how an obstacle can be, so when you find yourself face to face with a big obstruction, do not become discouraged. Later, you may change your point of view.

LEARN FROM WATER

The technique for reaching a goal is to follow the example of water. Water reaches its goal by flowing on.

What does water do when it comes upon a rock? It flows over or around it. When it comes to a precipice does it squeal, "Oh no! That's way too steep for me"? No. It goes right over the cliff. Does it hesitate even for a second? No. What happens when it comes to a hole? It fills it up and flows on.

On the other hand, what occurs when water does not move on? It gets stagnant. It is the same with us. If we let fear or indecision stop us, we get stagnant too.

The technique of flowing on like water works especially well when we are afraid to make a decision. How many times have we been afraid to act? How many times has fear left us frozen like a lizard? When we are afraid, the worst thing we can do is nothing. Just get started.

No matter what the situation is, after it has been thoroughly thought out, it is essential to form a decision and to act. When we do not act, we get stuck. At these times we can observe the example of water and flow on.

THE TECHNIQUE IN ACTION

Give generously. Water gives without asking to be repaid.

Speak faithfully, like the flow of water that always goes toward the sea.

Govern gently. Though water moves with gentleness, it can overcome even the hardest obstacle.

Be adaptable. Water can fit what is square or what is round. It keeps its true nature in any circumstance.

Take action opportunely. Water freezes in the winter and melts in the spring. *

– Ni, Hua Ching

Water dissolves things. Let it dissolve your obstacles. Look at any form of running water. Fix your gaze on a fountain. Sit at the seashore. Lie on a river bank. Gaze at rain and learn to be like water, continuously flowing on.

---

* *The Book of Changes and the Unchanging Truth,* College of Tao and Traditional Chinese Healing, Publisher

If you do not have a natural source, then turn on a garden hose. Use a faucet. Do it in the shower. Stare at running water and move on.

Staring at flowing water helps us bypass the old part of our thinking that gets stuck. It helps us get in touch with the part of us that is free and liquid. No matter how frozen we may be, there is a place inside that has mobility. Behind every obstruction is a great opening, a great opportunity. Let running water lead us there.

1. Write your goal at the top of a blank sheet of paper.

2. Draw three circles under the goal. In each circle, write one obstacle that lies between you and your goal.

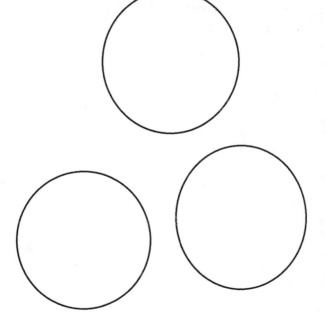

3. Go to the ocean, a stream, a lake, a river, a waterfall...any form of flowing water. Mentally place your obstacles from #2 in the water. Throw them in like rocks and watch what the water does. Choose which one you want to identify with: The rocks or the water. Let the water teach you to flow on.

4. Spend 10 minutes staring at water. Then use this memory in the future. Whenever you run up against an obstacle, ask yourself, "What would water do now?"

5. Write down three insights you had about reaching your goal.

Expert Advice

All of the expert advice offered by the volunteer leaders interviewed for this book could not be included in the main text. More of their seasoned suggestions can be found on the following pages.

Use this information like a round-table of experts. Every successful person has taken help from a group of experts.

It is not always easy to be the person in charge. When the going gets rough, wouldn't it be wonderful to sit down with someone who has been through the same thing? Wouldn't it help to have the benefit of experts who have walked this road before?

When you feel this way, read over the expert advice. Every idea has been tested by someone in a similar position to your own.

WAYS TO ATTRACT VOLUNTEERS

"Ask, and ye shall receive."

— New Testament

1. People volunteer if you ask.

2. If you are having fun, they will want to participate. If you think it is hard, so will they.

3. Have the conviction that whatever you touch will flourish. Carry the image of victory in your heart.

4. Do people want to get hooked into hard work? No! Do they jump at opportunities to surrender their time? No! Do they feel drawn to situations that generate gratifying feelings in them? Yes!

5. Professionals like to volunteer expertise in their field.

6. When three people meet with someone it is flattering and also hard for that person to turn down three people.

7. When asking people to volunteer, make them feel not just anyone could do it. They like to feel special.

8. Offer training. Volunteers see it as an opportunity to increase their skills and benefit professionally.

9. Provide a safe place to learn difficult skills: Writing, computer skills, advertising, by-laws preparation. For many people, volunteering leads to successful employment. The federal government stresses volunteer work on job applications. Develop a way for volunteers to develop the skills they want.

10. Contact people in transition through employment agencies, divorce attorneys, long term tourists.

11. Approach people who like to

make contacts. When people are new to a community, they like to meet people. Realtors, sales people, singles groups, teen groups. Some schools require seniors to volunteer. Rotary and Junior League offer their services to other non-profit groups.

12. Let volunteers recruit volunteers. Serve tea and have them share their experiences.

13. Hold training sessions to teach volunteers to talk about your organization. Encourage them to share their experiences wherever they go, e.g., meetings, errands, parties. Their enthusiasm will sell it.

14. People like to be with people they admire. Ask a local celebrity to come to a volunteer meeting, or make a public service announcement.

15. Have a "people person" around to draw others in. Everyone enjoys being around a positive person.

16. To attract young people, form a "Youth Leadership Training Program." Encourage them by saying, "Just try it!"

17. Find out what people need, then offer the work in a way that will appeal to them and fulfill their desire.

18. Use past presidents of the organization to serve as a personnel committee.

19. Be passionate. You must believe in your cause.

20. If you are afraid to ask, people sense it. If you feel needy or burdened, they sense that too. Fear and enthusiasm cannot occupy the mind at the same time.

21. Be honest from the beginning about what you want volunteers to do. What is the time commitment? What resources are available? What help can they expect?

22. Be flexible and accommodating. The task is more important than the hours.

23. Be very specific. Create short-term, project related tasks, e.g., "Will you canvas 8 houses?"

24. Time is not the issue. People will make time for things that make them feel good. Emphasize the good feeling they will get. Motivation is the key.

25. Ask a busy person.

26. See more people. An average sales ratio is 10:1. If you ask ten people, one will say "Yes." Consider the other nine as potential future volunteers. Or, think of it this way: It takes ten "No's" to get a "Yes." Each person who says "No" puts you that much closer to a "Yes."

27. The executive director can continually be out and about, infecting the public with "good vibrations."

MANAGEMENT TIPS

"The mark of a successful organization is not whether or not it has problems. It is whether it has the same problems it had last year."

— John Foster Dulles

1. The manager's job is to train, motivate and inspire.

2. Find a staff person who can unlock each individual's special needs and wants.

3. Look for what motivates people. What would make them want to do this?

4. "Feeling good" means different things to different people. Find it for each one.

5. People are what they are. Accept

what they can do.

6. Being a manager is not being an autocrat. Being a manager is being a servant.

7. Allow room for volunteers to change and grow. If you put them in a box, they leave you.

8. Identify exactly what results you want. People appreciate knowing what to expect. Whenever possible, create forms with job descriptions that tell them exactly what they are to do.

9. Challenge people by defining the need and asking them to find a way to fulfill it.

10. Volunteers need to know the hierarchy. Who they report to, check with, etc.

11. Orientations for volunteers are important. Asking someone to volunteer without an orientation

could short-sell the organization.

12. At orientations, introduce staff and board members, give the history and philosophy and explain current projects. Also, give specific information about the new volunteer's task.

13. Introduce them to people who have done the same work before.

14. Provide them with reports from the past.

15. Give prizes to long-time volunteers in order to get their reports turned in.

16. Be organized. Plan ahead. Do not waste anyone's time.

17. Make your goal very clear. Never take for granted that people understand what you are trying to do.

18. Paid staff must understand that it is a volunteer organization. They should feel, "I am lucky to have this

job. I would volunteer for it."

19. The paid staff must be willing to give up control. They should not be afraid to depend on volunteers.

20. Volunteers need to feel they are powerful and that they have a voice.

21. Remember that volunteers want to be social. They want to work with people. Organize the work around this.

22. Design programs and plans around getting people together.

23. Meetings should be short and inspiring.

24. An organization which cheats its volunteers of self-fulfillment, eventually cheats itself of prosperity.

25. Ruling with an iron hand is likely to produce rapid turnover of volunteers and weak commitment.

WAYS TO KEEP VOLUNTEERS

"Appreciate me now and avoid the rush."

– ©Ashleigh Brilliant

1. The paid staff should be trained to appreciate volunteers.

2. Everyone who comes in, even for just one day, should be made to feel a part of the team.

3. The executive director must make time to thank, nurture and give attention to volunteers.

4. Appreciation must be sincere. Volunteers can see through dishonesty faster than anyone.

5. Everyone wants to be heard and seen.

6. Treat them like they are staff, not "just volunteers."

7. Treat each person individually.

8. Identify what each person needs and give it. People volunteer in order to get their own needs met.

9. Appreciation is an immediate reward system. Do not make volunteers wait until they have put in 1000 hours. Everyday they should receive some sort of reward.

10. Give feedback on their work.

11. Keep them informed verbally, not just with newsletters.

12. Hold pot lucks for staff and volunteers.

13. If a regular volunteer goes away on a trip, give him or her a big send-off.

14. Acknowledge birthdays.

15. On holidays, give volunteers the same gifts and cards you give the paid staff.

16. Post names and photos on a bulletin board announcing, "Meet our volunteer, John Bedford."

17. Send flowers when someone gets sick.

18. "Thank you" parties are a great way to say, "Thank you and please help us again."

19. Sponsor picnics for volunteers and their families.

20. Write articles about them in your magazine or flyer.

21. Invite them to lunch with staff.

22. Be happy to see them come.

23. Treat everyone with respect.

ADVICE ON OVERCOMING OBSTACLES

"The degree of success is proportional to the number of obstacles overcome."

– A Law of Social Physics

1. Rotate positions so people do not get burned out.

2. Create new challenges. Do not keep volunteers doing something just because they are good at it. Let them grow.

3. Flow on like water.

4. Listen to music.

5. Go for a walk alone in nature.

6. When volunteers feel overwhelmed or burdened, joyfully give them

permission to not do the task. Simply giving this permission is often enough to relieve the burden.

7. Exercise your mind, body and spirit.

8. Call a meeting of your co-workers and ask for help.

9. Do not deliberate too long. Form decisions quickly and then act. The more time you spend making a decision, the more doubts arise, making it more and more difficult to act.

10. Extra effort is required at the very end. Have you seen how much energy it takes for an Olympic runner to cross the finish line?

FINAL EXERCISE #22

1. Did you get what you wanted from *To Lead Is To Serve*?

2. How are you different in the end than you were in the beginning?

The steps to success outlined above are there to be taken – step by step by step. The reward is worthy of your effort. Will you walk along?

Index

To Lead Is To Serve
$14.95

Discounts:
10 books = 10% off
25 books = 25% off

Video Series also available!
Learn how successful volunteer leaders
achieve the results you want.
$29.95

For information about products and
Shar McBee's keynote speeches:

1-800-814-8827